The Courts
and
Higher Education

john s. brubacher

the courts
and
higher education

Jossey-Bass Inc., Publishers
615 Montgomery Street • San Francisco • 1971

THE JOSSEY-BASS SERIES IN HIGHER EDUCATION

HAROLD L. HODGKINSON
University of California, Berkeley

Special editor for
Foundations of American Higher Education

Preface

Higher education in this country has been shaped by many forces—church, legislature, industry, commerce, and the like. Except for the Dartmouth College case little attention has been paid to the way in which the courts have been a factor in molding our colleges and universities. However, since 1960, during the decade of student unrest, the courts increasingly have been called on to arbitrate matters affecting educational policy. It is time, therefore, that those responsible for policy in higher education become acquainted with what the courts are saying, and have been saying, about the academic community.

American colleges and universities have a tradition of autonomy. They merit this autonomy because they are experts in higher education, and who is to judge expertise adequately but experts themselves? Consequently faculty and administration have enjoyed a large measure of discretion in such matters as setting admission and graduation requirements, selecting the curriculum, and disciplining students. Nearly every exercise of expertise on the campus has two aspects. Was there authority to act and, if so, was it wisely exercised? The courts have long been accustomed to examining the first question but have been wary about examining the second. This makes sense. Discretion is a question of scholarly expertise known best to the faculty and administration. In the past decade, however, courts have been increasingly tempted to review questions of discretion as well as those of authority.

Preface

The occasion for judicial prying into discretionary matters has grown out of accentuated public interest in civil liberties. As never before, courts are applying the principles of the First, Fifth, and Fourteenth Amendments to the transaction of academic affairs. Take the due process clause of the First and Fourteenth Amendments as an illustration. Dismissing a student used to be a simple matter within the autonomous discretion of the dean or faculty disciplinary committee. But now the courts may review this discretion both procedurally and substantively. Procedurally they inquire whether the student had a fair hearing, and substantively they examine whether college rules on discipline are reasonable. This review amounts to an important reduction in the traditional autonomy of the college or university. How much further is this encroachment likely to go? Obviously those engaged in higher education cannot surrender these powers to the exclusive jurisdiction of the courts. They must acquaint themselves, therefore, with the impact the courts are exerting on the campus. It is to this end that *The Courts and Higher Education* is dedicated.

The reader should be mindful of several cautions. No claim is made that a particular decision is followed throughout the country. Neither do all the cases come from appellate courts; indeed a few are still on their way there. Also, there is no inclusion of cases involving elementary and secondary schools even though they may be analogous to cases involving universities. To dip into this area would enlarge this study to unmanageable proportions. Finally, *The Courts and Higher Education* is designed to broaden the views of personnel in higher education, but it does not pretend to make them their own lawyers.

Bridgeport, Connecticut
October 1970

JOHN S. BRUBACHER

Contents

Contents

Contents

The Courts
and
Higher Education

ONE

Students

Right to Higher Education

Though higher education is currently generously provided and widely patronized, for the most part the patron has the option of taking advantage of the opportunities. Whether an adolescent in his late teens and still a minor can demand higher education as a right therefore raises an interesting question, one which was the issue in Esteb v. Esteb.[1] In that case a decree of divorce had made certain provisions for the support of the mother and her two minor daughters. After the divorce one of the daughters began attending college, and the mother then tried to have the divorce decree modified to provide an extra allowance for this unforeseen expense. The executrix of the father's estate opposed this expense as unnecessary.

[1] 138 Wash. 174–244 P. 264 (1926). Note: Most state supreme court decisions are reported both locally and regionally. Thus Esteb v. Esteb is reported not only in Volume 138 of the Washington State reports but in Volume 244 of the collected reports of a group of Pacific states. Other regional reports are designated as "A" for Atlantic states, "N.E." for northeastern states, "N.W." for northwestern states, "S.E." for southeastern, "S" for southern, and "S.W." for southwestern. The abbreviation "2nd" indicates the second series of the reporter system. A number of New York reports appear under the notation "N.Y.S.," the "S" meaning "supplement," which reports decisions of the lower courts. There are three systems of reports for the federal courts: "Fed. Supp." for the federal district courts, "Fed." for the circuit court of appeals, and "U.S." for the Supreme Court.

1

The Courts and Higher Education

The question of what is necessary for a minor has a long history. In ancient times Solon excused Athenian youths from maintaining their parents in their old age if their parents had failed to train them in some vocation when they were young. In early Anglo-American law a child could legally claim as necessities only food, shelter, and clothing. Strikingly, education was not regarded as a necessity. By the nineteenth century, however, this narrow rule of law had been modified, as attested by the Washington court:

Probably the earliest reported case in this country involving the question as to whether a college education is a necessity is Middlebury College v. Chandler, . . .[2] where a suit was brought to recover from the father tuition and other bills which represented a charge for his minor son, as a student at the college. This case appears to be authority and is referred to by nearly all text writers upon the question. The court there refused to hold that a college education was a necessary, but the court's reasoning for its holding is very interesting:

"The practical meaning of the term [necessaries] has always been in some measure relative, having reference as well to what may be called the conventional necessities of others in the same walks of life with the infant as to his own pecuniary condition and other circumstances. Hence a good, common school education, at the least, is now fully recognized as one of the necessaries for an infant. Without it he would lack an acquisition which would be common among his associates; he would suffer in his subsequent influence and usefulness in society and would ever be liable to suffer in his transactions of business. Such an education is, moreover, essential to the intelligent discharge of civil, political, and religious duties.

"But it is obvious that the more extensive attainments in literature and science must be viewed in a light somewhat different. Though they tend greatly to elevate and adorn personal character, are a source of much private enjoyment, and may justly be expected to prove of public utility, yet in refer-

[2] 16 Vt. 683 (1844).

ence to men in general they are far from being necessary in a legal sense. The mass of our citizens pass through life without them. I would not be understood as making any allusion to professional studies or to the education and training which is requisite to the knowledge and practice of mechanic arts. These partake of the nature of apprenticeships and stand on peculiar grounds of reason and policy. I speak only of the regular and full course of collegiate study, for such was the course upon which the defendant professedly entered. Now it does not appear that extraneous circumstances existed in the defendant's case, such as wealth or station in society, or that he exhibited peculiar indications of genius or talent, which would suggest the fitness and expediency of a college education for him more than for the generality of youth in community."

Since that time many cases have arisen concerning a minor's right to vocational education in commercial or industrial arts. The courts have found it difficult to lay down any general rules here. What is necessary, therefore, is not absolute but rather is relative to the minor's "condition in life, to the habits and pursuits of the place in which and the people among whom he lives, and to the changes in those habits and pursuits occurring in the progress of society."[3] If a college education fulfills these conditions, it is necessary.

In Esteb v. Esteb the court adjudicated that such an education was necessary. It thus pushed one step further the evolution of a minor's right to an education:

Applying the rule as stated by the courts and the text writers, it will be seen that the question of what sort of an education is necessary, being a relative one, the court should determine this in a proper case from all the facts and circumstances. Nor should the court be restricted to the station of the minor in society but should, in determining this fact, take into consideration the progress of society and the attendant require-

[3] 16 Vt. 683 (1844).

ments upon the citizens of today. The rule in Middlebury College v. Chandler . . . was clearly based upon conditions which existed at that time. . . . But conditions have changed greatly in almost a century that has elapsed since that time. Where the college graduate of that day was the exception, today such a person may almost be said to be the rule. The law in an attempt to keep up with the progress of society has gradually placed minimum standards for attendance upon public schools and even provides punishment for those parents who fail to see that their children receive at least such minimum education. That it is the public policy of the state that a college education should be had, if possible, by all its citizens, is made manifest by the fact that the state of Washington maintains so many institutions of higher learning at public expense. It cannot be doubted that the minor who is unable to secure a college education is generally handicapped in pursuing most of the trades or professions of life, for most of those with whom he is required to compete will be possessed of that greater skill and ability which comes from such an education.

It seems to be contended that the minor in this case should be content with a commercial education, and it is argued that since she is a graduate of the Lincoln High School, that fact demonstrates that she is able to earn her own living and should no longer be a charge upon her father. But the record discloses that she has no aptitude for commercial work. It also appears that she completed her high school course in a little more than one-half the time usually taken because of her genius for that class of work. It would seem, then, that she is not only unfitted for commercial life but that she is exceptionally well fitted for her chosen vocation [teaching].

Does this case mean that any father can be compelled to give his child a college education? Suppose the father decides to spend his money in some other fashion than on his child's college education? It is not likely as long as the child is under the custody of the father. In Esteb the mother had custody, and she decided in favor of a college education. Therefore, although the case is a significant extension of a long line of cases, one must be careful not to stretch it too far.

Race

Nearly everyone is acquainted with the move to desegregate the public schools of the country as a result of the famous case of Brown v. Board of Education.[4] Few, however, realize that precedents for that decision were first laid down in the field of higher education. For decades policy was ruled by the case of Plessy v. Ferguson,[5] which sanctioned separate schools for blacks and whites as long as their facilities were equal. But just what is the quality of this equality? During the depression of the 1930s a notable case reached the courts, challenging the "separate but equal" doctrine. In Missouri *ex rel.* Gaines v. Canada[6] a black applied for admission to the University of Missouri Law School and was refused. He had a bachelor's degree from Lincoln University, which Missouri had established for the black race. The Missouri legislature had declared its intent to establish a school of law on the Lincoln campus, but the actualization of this intent was left to the discretion of the curators of the university. They had the choice either to erect a law school or to send the applicant to a neighboring state university which accepted blacks. Gaines was not satisfied with this substitute in spite of the fact that the law schools out of state were of a high quality and had curricula similar to that of the University of Missouri Law School.

He carried his objection to the United States Supreme Court, where Chief Justice Charles Evans Hughes, speaking for the court, said:

We think that these matters are beside the point. The basic consideration is not as to what sort of opportunities other states provide or whether they are as good as those in Missouri but as to what opportunities Missouri itself furnishes to white students and denies to Negroes solely upon the ground

[4] 367 U.S. 483 (1954).
[5] 163 U.S. 537 (1899).
[6] 305 U.S. 337 (1938).

5

of color. The admissibility of laws separating the races in the enjoyment of privileges afforded by the state rests wholly upon the equality of the privileges which the laws give to the separated groups within the state. The question here is not of a duty of the state to supply legal training, or of the quality of the training which it does supply, but of its duty when it provides such training to furnish it to the residents of the state upon the basis of an equality of right. By the operation of the laws of Missouri a privilege has been created for white law students which is denied to Negroes by reason of their race. The white resident is afforded legal education within the state; the Negro resident having the same qualifications is refused it there and must go outside the state to obtain it. That is a denial of the equality of legal right to the enjoyment of the privilege which the state has set up, and the provision for the payment of tuition fees in another state does not remove the discrimination.

The equal protection of the laws is "a pledge of the protection of equal laws." . . . Manifestly, the obligation of the state to give the protection of equal laws can be performed only where its laws operate, that is, within its own jurisdiction. . . . That obligation is imposed by the Constitution upon the states severally as governmental entities—each responsible for its own laws establishing the rights and duties of persons within its borders. It is an obligation the burden of which cannot be cast by one state upon another, and no state can be excused from performance by what another state may do or fail to do.

Complementing Missouri *ex rel.* Gaines v. Canada is Sweatt v. Painter.[7] In this instance the State of Texas established a separate law school for blacks. The plaintiff, however, was not satisfied with the equality of the facilities in spite of the fact that professors from the University of Texas were to lecture there. Agreeing with him, the court stated,

[7] 339 U.S. 629 (1950).

6

Students

In terms of number of the faculty, variety of courses and opportunity for specialization, size of the student body, scope of the library, availability of law review, and similar activities, the University of Texas Law School is superior. What is more important, the University of Texas Law School possesses to a far greater degree those qualities which are incapable of objective measurement but which make for greatness in a law school. Such qualities, to name but a few, include reputation of the faculty, experience of the administration, position and influence of the alumni, standing in the community, traditions, and prestige. It is difficult to believe that one who had a free choice between these law schools would consider the question closely.

Moreover, although the law is a highly learned profession, we are well aware that it is an intensely practical one. The law school, the proving ground for legal learning and practice, cannot be effective in isolation from the individuals and institutions with which the law interacts. Few students and no one who has practiced law would choose to study in an academic vacuum, removed from the interplay of ideas and the exchange of views with which the law is concerned. The law school to which Texas is willing to admit petitioner excludes from its student body members of the racial groups which number 85 per cent of the population of the state and include most of the lawyers, witnesses, jurors, judges, and other officials with whom petitioner will inevitably be dealing when he becomes a member of the Texas Bar. With such a substantial and significant segment of society excluded, we cannot conclude that the education offered petitioner is substantially equal to that which he would receive if admitted to the University of Texas Law School.

That the courts have not been fooled by subterfuges regarding the equal protection of the laws is notable. Impelled by the Gaines decision the Oklahoma legislature amended its statutes to provide for the admission of blacks at the white state university but

7

on a segregated basis. In McLaurin v. Oklahoma State Regents,[8] the plaintiff was required to sit apart at a designated desk in an anteroom adjoining the main classroom, to sit at another designated desk on the mezzanine of the library, and to sit at yet another designated table in the cafeteria, which he had to use at a different time from other students. The court brushed these requirements aside as inconsistent with the equal protection of the laws.

It may be argued that appellant will be in no better position when these restrictions are removed, for he may still be set apart by his fellow students. This we think irrelevant. There is a vast difference—a Constitutional difference—between restrictions imposed by the state which prohibit the intellectual commingling of students and the refusal of individuals to commingle where the state presents no such bar. . . . The removal of the state restrictions will not necessarily abate individual and group predilections, prejudices, and choices. But at the very least, the state will not be depriving appellant of the opportunity to secure acceptance by his fellow students on his own merits.

Student Protest and Disruption

More or less violent student disturbances have a history extending back to medieval times. Never have they been so widespread, however, as in the past decade. The activists of this period in contrast to the silent generation of the preceding decade were motivated by a very sensitive social conscience. The war in Vietnam on the one hand and a sluggish academic establishment on the other stirred one student protest after another. Most colleges and universities have rules to keep student disorder in hand, but breaches of the rules have led to suspensions and even expulsions. To gain redress for these disciplinary measures, students have had recourse to the courts. Some leading cases illustrate where the lines were drawn.

[8] 339 U.S. 637 (1950).

Students

One of the most notorious cases of student rioting occurred at Columbia University during the spring of 1968. The students claimed to have two grievances. One was that the university was planning to build a new gymnasium partly on land taken from a neighboring recreation space for nearby Harlem blacks. The other was that the university was putting its expertise at the service of the federal government for war purposes. Addressing their grievances through normal channels to the university administration, the students received no serious consideration. To command attention for their complaints they occupied buildings on the campus until forced to yield them by the police.

As part of his effort to cope with the disturbances President Grayson Kirk of Columbia appointed a Joint Committee on Disciplinary Affairs comprised of faculty, students, and administrators. This committee decided to discipline all involved by placing them on probation, but a probation which would not entail loss of financial aid or denial of participation in political activities of the university. Several students, designated as subject to this discipline, were called on to appear before the dean to indicate how they would plead—guilty, not guilty, or stand mute to the charges. Failure to appear by a given date was cause for suspension. The designated students failed to appear except by attorney, a substitute the dean refused to accept. Furthermore, they continued with rioting activities and were arrested. After their arrest they again failed to appear before the dean on the ground that the charge of criminal trespass must be disposed of first. If they appeared before the dean first, they might be called upon to give information which could be used to incriminate them in the trespass proceedings, a course of events which would violate their Fifth Amendment guarantees. In any event the final date for their appearance before the dean passed without their showing up, and consequently they were suspended. The students' attempt to prevent their suspension resulted in the case of Grossner v. Trustees of Columbia University.[9]

The plaintiffs rested their case on the First, Fifth, and Fourteenth Amendments of the Constitution. The court came to grips

[9] 287 Fed. Supp. 535 (1968).

9

with the principal argument, violation of the First Amendment guarantee of freedom of expression, by stating that:

Our highest court has made clear in the labors of a long generation that the First Amendment mandate protecting free expression "must be taken as a command of the broadest scope that explicit language, read in the context of a liberty-loving society, will allow." . . . The court has insisted steadily on the "principle that debate on public issues should be uninhibited, robust, and wide open. . . ." It has also made clear, however, the gross error of believing that every kind of conduct (however nonverbal and physically destructive or obstructive) must be treated simply as protected "speech" because those engaged in it intend to express some view or position. . . . Similarly, the court has rejected the notion that "everyone with opinions or beliefs to express may do so at any time or any place." . . . Without such inescapably necessary limits, the First Amendment would be a self-destroying license for "peaceful expression" by the seizure of streets, buildings, and offices by mobs, large or small, driven by motives (and toward objectives) that different viewers might deem "good or bad." . . . It is such a license plaintiffs claim when they state the basic premise of their lawsuit as follows:

"Plaintiffs maintain, consistent with the American tradition of democratic and legal confrontation, that the nonviolent occupation of five buildings of Columbia University for less than one week in the circumstances of this case is fully protected by the First Amendment guarantees of the right to petition government for the redress of grievances, . . . to assemble, and to speak. Plaintiffs maintain that the nonviolent occupation of the buildings was absolutely necessary to breathe life into the First Amendment principle that government institutions should reflect the will of the people and that this interest must prevail under any balancing test against the inconvenience to defendant Columbia University in having five of its buildings occupied by students for approximately one week."

Embellishing such untenable propositions, plaintiffs (or,

10

*more fairly, the sixteen attorneys who sign their brief)' proceed
to argue that the rhetoric and the tactics of the American Revolution are the guides by which judges are to construe the First
Amendment. The "rule of law," they explain, must not be
overrated: "Had Americans agreed that the rule of law, however despotic, must always prevail, had the Americans felt that
dropping the tea in the harbor was going too far, had the
Americans not focused on fundamental principles, this country
might still be a colony today." The message, insofar as it is in-
telligible, possibly means that a tea party today, if nothing else
could achieve repeal of a hated tax, would be protected by the
First Amendment. Or possibly it means something else. Whatever it is meant to mean, and whatever virtues somebody might
think such ideas might have in other forms, arguments like
this are at best useless (at worst deeply pernicious) nonsense
in courts of law. . . .*

*It is surely nonsense . . . to argue that a court of law
should subordinate the "rule of law" in favor of more "fundamental principles" of revolutionary action designed forcibly to
oust government, courts and all. But this self-contradictory
sort of theory . . . is ultimately at the heart of plaintiffs' case.
And so it is not surprising that plaintiffs' efforts to implement
the theory have led them to champion a series of propositions
of unsound constitutional law.*

The court made short shrift of plaintiffs' Fifth Amendment
plea. It viewed appearance before the dean as a procedural affair.
The plaintiffs were merely to indicate whether they accepted disciplinary probation or wished to contest it in further proceedings,
and nothing they would have said could have been self-incrimina-
tory in the trial. Moreover, "nothing in the Fifth Amendment or
any other amendment," the judge said, "supports plaintiffs' contention that they . . . had a right to nullify the disciplinary procedures simply by announcing that they would not appear even to
'plead' to the charges."

The students had also hoped to buttress their case by an
appeal to the Fourteenth Amendment. To invoke its due process

clause they had to overcome the fact that Columbia was a private university. They pointed out that Columbia officials were engaged in "state action." The alleged state action consisted of the fact that over 40 per cent of the university budget for the preceding two years was derived from public funds, a considerable portion of which went for defense purposes. The court held that much more was necessary than the receipt of public money to prove state action. The point is not the source of funds but whether there was an interedependence between Columbia University and the government. As the court found no such connection, it became unnecessary to examine whether due process had been exercised in suspending the plaintiffs.

On a southern campus students also thought college disciplinary regulations had a "chilling" effect on First Amendment freedoms. In that case, Hammond v. South Carolina State College,[10] the court held that they did. Some three hundred students had assembled on the campus to express their disapproval of certain college practices. They later claimed they did so in an orderly and peaceful fashion. The college administration, however, regarded the meeting as noisy and disorderly and therefore summoned the plaintiffs to appear before the college disciplinary committee. After facing charges they were summarily expelled under a rule in the student handbook prohibiting student demonstrations without prior approval of the college administration.

Plaintiffs sought a court order to restrain the college authorities from carrying out their expulsion. They contended that this college rule was a prior restraint on their exercise of First Amendment freedoms. They argued that these freedoms are not genuine if permission must be obtained to exercise them. Siding with the plaintiffs the court declared:

> *These rights of the First Amendment, including the right to peaceably assemble, are not to be restricted except upon the showing of a clear and present danger, of riot, disorder, or immediate threat to public safety, peace, or order.*

[10] 281 Fed. Supp. 280 (1968).

. . . "Only the gravest abuses, endangering paramount interests, give occasion for permissible limitation." . . . Conduct which involves activities such as picketing and marching, however, are a departure from the exercise of the rights in pristine form and they do not receive the same degree of freedom. . . . It has been argued to me that Rule 1 of the student handbook as it is written is a previous restraint upon these rights and as such it is unlawful and must be struck down as being "incompatible with the guarantees of the First Amendment." . . . I am persuaded that Rule 1 is on its face a prior restraint on the right to freedom of speech and the right to assemble. The rule does not purport to prohibit assemblies which have qualities that are unacceptable to responsible standards of conduct: it prohibits "parades, celebrations, and demonstrations" without prior approval without any regard to limiting its proscription to assemblies involving misconduct or disruption of government activities or nonpeacable gatherings. On this ground I do not feel that it is necessary to make a finding as to the nature of the demonstration.

Although the court in the Hammond case did not feel called upon to deal with how disorderly the students had been, this question has been the main point in other cases, and there is a notable division of judicial opinion. The division centers on how specific college and university regulations must be in defining the kind of disorder which may lead to suspension or expulsion of the student. The contrast of two federal cases is most informative.

The first case, Soglin v. Kaufmann,[11] arose from an attempt by students to obstruct access to an off-campus recruiter for an industrial concern producing war materials. Plaintiffs, members of Students for a Democratic Society, were charged with misconduct and expelled. The word *misconduct* was not spelled out in the university statutes, and the students took exception to being expelled on the basis of what they alleged to be unconstitutionally vague language. Federal Judge Doyle, before whom the case was tried,

[11] 295 Fed. Supp. 978 (1968).

13

sided with the plaintiffs, citing the familiar rule of law: "[A] statute which either forbids or requires the doing of an act in terms so vague that men of common intelligence must necessarily guess its meaning and differ as to its application violates the first essential of due process of law." The judge also found this rule of law embodied in a statement of the American Association of University Professors to the effect that "Disciplinary proceedings should be instituted only for violation of standards of conduct defined in advance and published through such means as a student handbook or a generally available body of university regulations. Offenses should be as clearly defined as possible and such vague phrases as *undesirable conduct* or *conduct injurious to the best interests of the institution*[12] should be avoided." Applying these precedents to the case the judge reasoned, "The constitutional doctrines of vagueness and overbreadth are applicable, in some measure, to the standard or standards to be applied by the university in disciplining its students, and . . . a regime in which the term *misconduct* serves as the sole standard violates the due process clause of the Fourteenth Amendment by reason of its vagueness, or, in the alternative, violates the First Amendment as embodied in the Fourteenth by reason of its vagueness and overbreadth."

The university tried to meet the charge of vagueness by referring to another passage in its statutes which declared that students had the right to freedom of speech, peaceable assembly, petition, and association as long as they did not disrupt the operations of the university. The judge waved this evidence aside as being merely a declaration of student rights rather than being a regulation of their conduct since the passage contained no prohibitions, compulsions, or no sanctions. Although the judge did not sympathize with this aspect of the university's case, he did realize that it would be a serious inconvenience for the university to switch suddenly from a policy of meting out discipline under a vague directive to one where the directive is spelled out in much more detail. Since this transition would take some time, the court refused to give the immediate in-

---

[12] "Statement on the Academic Freedom of Students," *American Association of University Professors Bulletin*, 1965, *51*, 447, 449.

14

junctive relief prayed for by plaintiffs, which would have left the university defenseless for the time being in the regulation of student conduct. While the university worked out new regulations, consistent with the court's opinion, plaintiffs were left to seek judicial review, case by case, of disciplinary measures taken under the existing system.

This case is interesting in light of the history of college and university disciplinary regulations. Throughout the colonial period and well into the nineteenth century institutions of higher learning had voluminous rules prescribing student conduct to the minutest detail. Nothing seemed too insignficant on which to legislate, from hours of study and play to the cut of one's clothes and modes of courtesy. Early student disturbances seem to have been due in part to the oppressive spirit engendered by overregulation. Therefore, it was thought to be a great step forward when, toward the end of the nineteenth century, these rules were relaxed and sometimes discarded. The new policy was that if young men were treated like gentlemen they would behave like gentlemen. This optimistic view seemed to work well enough until the late 1950s, when there was an outbreak not only of civil disobedience and violent rioting but also of boorish manners and obscene speech. In arriving at his decision, Doyle was mindful of this history. He noted that

> *historically, universities and colleges . . . have enjoyed wide latitude in student discipline. Various "models" of the relationship between the university and its students have been employed by the courts for the purpose of determining the legal attributes of the relationship: parent-child* (in loco parentis); *owner-tenant; parties to a contract. . . . Whatever the model or combination of models employed, the dominant pattern has been judicial nonintervention in the discipline of students by faculty, administrators, school boards, trustees, or regents.*

> *In recent years, however, courts have been increasingly disposed to intervene in school disciplinary situations involving major sanctions. This has been most marked when intervention has appeared necessary to assure that procedural due*

process is observed: for example, specification of charges, notice of hearing, and hearing. . . . But judicial intervention has not been confined to matters of procedural due process. The validity of substantive school rules [also] has been the subject of judicial scrutiny.

Indeed, in numerous contexts, the Supreme Court has assigned a special importance to First Amendment guarantees in the educational setting. . . .

Underlying these developments in the relationship of academic institutions to the courts has been a profound shift in the nature of American . . . colleges and universities and in the relationships between younger and older people. These changes seldom have been articulated in judicial decisions but they are increasingly reflected there. The facts of life have long since undermined the concepts, such as in loco parentis, *which have been invoked historically for conferring upon university authorities virtually limitless disciplinary discretion.*

I take notice that in the present day, expulsion from an institution of higher learning, or suspension for a period of time substantial enough to prevent one from obtaining academic credit for a particular term, may well be, and often is in fact, a more severe sanction than a monetary fine or a relatively brief confinement imposed by a court in a criminal proceeding.

The world is much with the modern state university. Some find this regrettable, mourning the passing of what is said to have been the old order. I do not share this view. But whether the developments are pleasing is irrelevant to the present issue. What is relevant is that the University of Wisconsin at Madison may continue to encompass functions and situations such as those which characterized a small liberal arts college of the early twentieth century (of which some no doubt exist today), but that it encompasses many more functions and situations which bear little or no resemblance to the "models" which appear to have underlain, and continue in some cases to underlie, judicial response to cases involving col-

16

lege or university discipline. What is relevant is that in today's world university disciplinary proceedings are likely to involve many forms of misconduct other than fraternity hazing or plagiarism, and that the sanctions imposed may involve consequences for a particular student more grave than those involved in some criminal court proceedings.

The contrasting case, Esteban v. Central Missouri State College,[13] arose from disturbances caused by an unruly mob on the campus. Two students joined in the disturbances and refused to disengage themselves when told to do so by members of the college staff. They were cited for disciplinary action and suspended for violation of college regulations, the most pertinent of which stated that participation in mass gatherings which might be considered as unruly or unlawful could result in dismissal from the college. Although the students were permitted to apply for readmission at a later semester, they instead brought suit to command readmission.

A number of legal issues were decided by Judge Harry Blackmun but the one of most interest in the light of Soglin v. Kaufmann was this:

[The regulations] are additionally attacked for vagueness and overbreadth and hence on substantive due process grounds. Some of the loyalty oath cases are cited and it is said that the regulations' word "unlawful" is only a legal conclusion and that their references to "unruly" and "spectators" and "which might be considered" are undefined and possess no standards. The regulations are likened to city ordinances which have been struck down when they lack sufficiency of definition. It is then argued that "young people should be told clearly what is right and what is wrong, as well as the consequences of their acts." . . . Finally, it is said that the regulations impinge and have a chilling effect upon First and Fourteenth amendment rights.

The answers to all this, we think, are several. First, the college's regulations, per se, do not appear to us to constitute

[13] 415 Fed. 2nd 1077 (1969).

17

the fulcrum of the plaintiffs' discomfiture. The charges against Esteban and Roberds did not even refer to the regulations. Roberds was disciplined because he had participated in the demonstrations in the face of specific warning delivered by personal interview with the dean. This was defiance of proper college authority. Esteban was disciplined because of his refusal to comply with an appropriate request by Dr. Meverden and because of his childish behavior and obscenity toward college officials. This, too, was defiance of proper college authority. There was no confusion or unawareness in either case. The exercise of common sense was all that was required. Each plaintiff knew the situation very well, knew what he was doing, and knew the consequences. Each, we might note, had had prior disciplinary experience. Their respective protestations of young and injured innocence have a hollow ring.

Secondly, we agree with Judge Hunter [in the court below] that it is not sound to draw an analogy between student discipline and criminal procedure, that the standard of conduct which a college seeks to impose must be one relevant to "a lawful mission, process or function of the educational institution," and that "certainly the regulation concerning mass demonstrations, reasonably interpreted, and as interpreted and applied by the college in the instant case to a participant in student mass demonstrations involving unlawful conduct such as the illegal blocking of a public highway and street, and the destruction of school property, is relevant to a lawful mission of the educational institution."

Thirdly, we do not find the regulation at all difficult to understand and we are positive the college student, who is appropriately expected to possess some minimum intelligence, would not find it difficult. It asks for the adherence to standards of conduct which befit a student and it warns of the danger of mass-involvement. We must assume Esteban and Roberds can read and that they possess some power of comprehension. Their difficulty was that they chose not to read or not to comprehend.

18

Fourthly, we see little basically or constitutionally wrong with flexibility and reasonable breadth rather than meticulous specificity in college regulations relating to conduct. Certainly these regulations are not to be compared with the criminal statute. They are codes of general conduct which those qualified and experienced in the field have characterized not as punishment but as part of the educational process itself and as preferably to be expressed in general rather than in specific terms. . . .

We agree with those courts which have held that a school has inherent authority to maintain order and to discipline students. . . . We further agree that a school has latitude and discretion in its formulation of rules and regulations and of general standards of conduct. . . .

Our attention has been called to the fact that Judge Doyle, in his recent opinion in Soglin v. Kaufmann, 295 Fed. Supp. 978 . . . expresses disagreement with the observations of Judge Hunter on this aspect of the case. To the extent that in this area Judge Doyle is in disagreement with Judge Hunter, we must respectfully disagree with Judge Doyle.

Let there be no misunderstanding as to our precise holding. We do not hold that any college regulation, however loosely framed, is necessarily valid. We do not hold that a school has the authority to require a student to discard any constitutional right. . . . We do hold that a college has the inherent power to promulgate rules and regulations; that it has power appropriately to protect itself and its property; that it may expect that its students adhere to generally accepted standards of conduct; that, as to these, flexibility and elbow room are to be preferred over specificity; . . . that school regulations are not to be measured by the standards which prevail for the criminal law and criminal procedure; and that the courts should interfere only where there is a clear case of constitutional infringement.

It was mentioned above how early campus regulations sometimes specified minuscule matters. In the past decade the cut of

19

male college students' hair has been an object of concern for college authorities, and some have laid down prescriptions for hair length. In doing so, they often have increased the students' discontent. Shortly after enrollment at Jefferson State Junior College, the two plaintiffs in Zachry v. Brown[14] were administratively withdrawn for failing to comply with a campus regulation prescribing permissible hair styles. Both plaintiffs were members of a student band which had adopted pageboy haircuts, a style not conforming to campus regulations. Plaintiffs contested the order for their withdrawal. The college admitted at the trial that neither plaintiff had been a disciplinary problem. Both, indeed, passed their college entrance examinations in the upper ten per cent of their class. Plaintiff Zachry, moreover, was a candidate for his class presidency and would probably have been elected if he had not been withdrawn. Defendants admitted that insistence on withdrawal was motivated solely by dislike for what the college considered exotic hair styling. The college made no allegation that this styling interfered with the discipline of the campus.

The court had no difficulty in finding for the plaintiffs.

The wide latitude permitted . . . the administrators of public colleges to classify students with respect to dress, appearance, and behavior must be respected and preserved by the courts. However, the equal protection clause of the Fourteenth Amendment prohibits classification upon an unreasonable basis. This court is of the firm opinion that the classification of male students attending Jefferson State Junior College by their hair style is unreasonable and fails to pass constitutional muster.

It needs to be emphasized that the defendants have not sought to justify such classification for moral and social reasons. The only reason stated upon the hearing of this case was their understandable personal dislike of long hair on men students. The requirement that these plaintiffs cut their hair to conform to normal or conventional styles is just as unreason-

[14] 299 Fed. Supp. 1360 (1967).

*able as would palpably be a requirement that all male students
of the college wear their hair down over their ears and collars.*

Dismissal Procedure

The courts have reviewed carefully the causes for which
students have been dismissed but they have given even closer scrutiny to the method of dismissal. There are two basic legal viewpoints regarding dismissal procedure. The older is expressed in Anthony v. Syracuse University.[15] A coed was peremptorily dismissed
without clear cause beyond that university authorities had learned
that she was a troublemaker in her sorority house and that they did
not regard her as a "typical Syracuse girl." In her complaint to the
court for reinstatement she alleged that her dismissal had been arbitrary. She claimed that customarily a student at the university es-
tablishes a contractual relationship under which, after compliance
with all reasonable rules of scholarship and deportment, she is entitled to pursue her selected course to completion.

The university contended that the coed's attendance was
strictly at the pleasure of the university and in support pointed to
the registration card which plaintiff had signed. This card stated
that attendance at the university was a privilege and not a right
and that in order to safeguard scholarship and a moral atmosphere,
the university reserved the right to require the withdrawal of any
student at any time for any reason. The plaintiff argued that this
regulation was not binding on her principally because it was contrary to public policy. Addressing itself to this point, the court held
that

> *the argument on public policy is based upon the theory
> that consent to such a regulation . . . amounts to a permis-
> sion given the university authorities to do an act which would
> necessarily injure the reputation of the student. Such injury to
> reputation, however, if it occurred, would be merely inciden-
> tal. As both parties argue, the relation between plaintiff and
> defendant was wholly contractual. It was voluntary in its in-*

[15] 231 N.Y.S. 435 (1928).

21

ception on both sides. A student is not required to enter the university, and may in fact, after entry, withdraw without reason at any time. The university need not accept as a student one desiring to become such. It may, therefore, limit the effect of such acceptance by express agreement, and thus retain the position of contractual freedom in which it stood before the student's course was entered upon. I can discover no reason why a student may not agree to grant to the institution an optional right to terminate the relations between them. The contract between an institution and a student does not differ in this respect from contracts of employment. . . .

The construction of the regulation may be material. The regulation, in my judgment, does not reserve to the defendant an absolute right to dismiss the plaintiff for any cause whatever. Its right to dismiss is limited, for the regulation must be read as a whole. The university may only dismiss a student for reasons falling within two classes, one in connection with safeguarding the university's ideals of scholarship, and the other in connection with safeguarding the university's moral atmosphere. When dismissing a student, no reason for dismissing need be given. The university must, however, have a reason, and that reason must fall within one of the two classes mentioned above. Of course, the university authorities have wide discretion in determining what situation does and what does not fall within the classes mentioned, and the courts would be slow indeed in disturbing any decision of the university authorities in this respect. . . .

When the plaintiff comes into court and alleges a breach of contract, the burden rests upon her to establish such breach. She must show that her dismissal was not for a reason within the terms of the regulation. The record here is meager on this subject. While no adequate reason was assigned by the university authorities for the dismissal, I find nothing in the record on which to base a finding that no such reason existed. She offered no testimony, either as to her character and relation with her college associates, or as to her scholarship and attention to her academic duties. The evidence discloses no reason for her dismissal not falling within the terms of the regulation. It follows, therefore, that the action fails.

The newer precedent on dismissal procedure is stated in Dixon v. Alabama State Board of Education.[16] The plaintiffs had been students in good standing at Alabama State College for Negroes. By prearranged plan they entered as a group into a publicly owned grill and asked to be served. Service was denied, and when the students refused to leave, the grill was closed and the police were called. After this incident they were expelled from the college. Since their expulsion was without notice, hearing, or appeal, they contended that they had been denied due process of law. As in Anthony v. Syracuse, the college claimed that notice and hearing were not required because of a State Board of Education regulation which stated that, just as a student might choose to withdraw from a particular college at any time for any personally-determined reason, the college might also at any time decline to continue to accept responsibility for the supervision and service to any student with whom the relationship had become unpleasant and difficult.

This federal court, however, said,

We do not read this provision to clearly indicate an intent on the part of the student to waive notice and a hearing before expulsion. If, however, we should so assume, it nonetheless remains true that the state cannot condition the granting of even a privilege upon the renunciation of the constitutional right to procedural due process. . . . Only private associations have the right to obtain a waiver of notice and hearing before depriving a member of a valuable right. And, even here, the right to notice and a hearing is so fundamental to the conduct of our society that the waiver must be clear and explicit. . . .

The precise nature of the private interest involved in this case is the right to remain at a public institution of higher

[16] 294 Fed. 2nd 150 (1961).

23

learning in which the plaintiffs were students in good stand-
ing. It requires no argument to demonstrate that education is
vital and, indeed, basic to civilized society. Without sufficient
education the plaintiffs would not be able to earn an adequate
livelihood, to enjoy life to the fullest, or to fulfill as com-
pletely as possible the duties and responsibilities of good citi-
zens. . . .

Turning then to the nature of the governmental power
to expel the plaintiffs, it must be conceded, as was held by
the district court, that the power is not unlimited and can-
not be arbitrarily exercised. Admittedly, there must be some
reasonable and constitutional ground for expulsion or the
courts would have a duty to require reinstatement. The pos-
sibility of arbitrary action is not excluded by the existence of
reasonable regulations. There may be arbitrary application of
the rule to the facts of a particular case. Indeed, that result is
well nigh inevitable when the board heard only one side of
the issue. In the disciplining of college students there are no
considerations of immediate danger to the public or of peril
to the national security which should prevent the board from
exercising at least the fundamental principles of fairness by
giving the accused students notice of the charges and an op-
portunity to be heard in their own defense. Indeed, the ex-
ample set by the board in failing so to do, if not corrected by
the courts, can well break the spirits of the expelled students
and of others familiar with the injustice, and do inestimable
harm to their education.

Aware that its conclusions were seemingly opposite those in
Anthony v. Syracuse, the court distinguished the two in that Syracuse was a private institution whereas Alabama State College for
Negroes was a public one. In spite of this distinction a dissenting
judge still thought that Anthony v. Syracuse expressed the weight
of authority and that the failure of the majority to follow this precedent amounted to a failure to understand the nature and mission
of higher education. Expanding this idea the dissenting judge declared:

Students

*Everyone who has dealt with schools knows that it is
necessary to make many rules governing the conduct of those
who attend them, which do not reach the concept of crimi-
nality but which are designed to regulate the relationship between school management and the student based upon practical and ethical considerations which the courts know very little
about and with which they are not equipped to deal. To extend the injunctive power of federal courts to the problems of
day to day dealings between school authority and student discipline and morale is to add to the now crushing responsibilities of federal functionaries the necessity of qualifying as a
Gargantuan aggregation of wet nurses or baby sitters. I do not
believe that a balanced consideration of the problem with
which we are dealing contemplates any such extreme attitude.*

Nevertheless, the majority of the court concluded:

*We are confident that precedent as well as a most fun-
damental constitutional principle support our holding that due
process requires notice and . . . hearing before a student at a
tax-supported college is expelled for misconduct.*

*For the guidance of the parties in the event of further
proceedings, we state our views on the nature of the notice
and hearing required by due process. . . . The notice should
contain a statement of the specific charges and grounds which,
if proven, would justify expulsion under the regulations of the
board of education. The nature of the hearing should vary depending upon the circumstances of the particular case. The
case before us requires something more than an informal interview with an administrative authority of the college. By its
nature, a charge of misconduct, as opposed to a failure to meet
the scholastic standards of the college, depends upon a collec-
tion of the facts concerning the charged misconduct, easily
colored by the point of view of the witnesses. In such circumstances, a hearing which gives the board or the administrative
authorities of the college an opportunity to hear both sides in
considerable detail is best suited to protect the rights of all*

25

involved. This is not to imply that a full-dress judicial hearing, with the right to cross-examine witnesses, is required. Such a hearing, with the attending publicity and disturbance of college activities, might be detrimental to the college's educational atmosphere and impractical to carry out. Nevertheless, the rudiments of an adversary proceeding may be preserved without encroaching upon the interests of the college. In the instant case, the student should be given the names of the witnesses against him and an oral or written report on the facts to which each witness testifies. He should also be given the opportunity to present to the board, or at least to an administrative official of the college, his own defense against the charges and to produce either oral testimony or written affidavits of witnesses in his behalf. If the hearing is not before the board directly, the results and findings of the hearing should be presented in a report open to the student's inspection. If these rudimentary elements of fair play are followed, . . . we feel that the requirements of due process of law will have been fulfilled.

In the next few years, as suspensions and expulsions mounted, the courts were inundated with cases like Dixon. As a result the Federal District Court for Western Missouri handed down a general order specifying judicial standards to apply to disciplinary cases in public tax-supported institutions of higher learning. The order not only elaborated the rules suggested by the judge in Dixon v. Alabama but it also gave them a substantive setting as well. Substantively the full bench noted that attendance at institutions of higher education is voluntary and therefore that students voluntarily assume all reasonable obligations imposed by these institutions. Moreover, these obligations are much higher than those imposed on the general citizenry by civil and criminal law. Among these they have the heightened obligation not to intentionally prevent a college or university from accomplishing its lawful purposes.

Student Publications

Student publications have often been a source of tension between students and administration. The tension usually arises because students want to proceed in the tradition of freedom of the press and yet do not have the maturity to do so. In Dickey v. Alabama State Board of Education[17] the editor of the Troy State College student paper proposed to write an editorial in support of President Frank Rose of the University of Alabama. On the latter campus students had instituted a program inviting off-campus speakers to address students on both sides of the theme "World in Revolution." Together with speakers like Dean Rusk were others like Stokely Carmichael and the communist Bettine Aptheker. Rose backed this program on grounds of academic freedom but in doing so incurred strong criticism from state legislators.

Plaintiff submitted his proposed editorial in support of the neighboring university president to his paper's faculty adviser who counseled against its publication. His English professor, however, approved it. He then took it to President Ralph Adams of Troy State College who ruled against its publication because it was critical of the governor and legislature of the state. The theory of this so-called "Adams rule" was that the college was a public institution and the governor and legislators acted as the owners. The newspaper could not criticize its owners, the president reasoned, especially since they controlled the allocation of funds to the college. Except for this objection the editorial was considered in good taste. Barred from publishing the article, the editor left the editorial space in his paper blank save for a caption "A Lament for Dr. Rose" and the word *censored* spread diagonally across the empty space. In addition he sent the editorial to a Montgomery newspaper. For these actions he was dismissed from the college and sought reinstatement.

The court directed the student's reinstatement with the following observations:

> It is basic in our law . . . that the privilege to communicate concerning a matter of public interest is embraced in the First Amendment right relating to freedom of speech and is constitutionally protected against infringement by state officials. The Fourteenth Amendment . . . protects these First

[17] 273 Fed. Supp. 613 (1967).

27

Amendment rights from state infringement, . . . and these First Amendment rights extend to school children and students insofar as unreasonable rules are concerned. West Virginia State Board of Education v. Barnette, 319 U.S. 624.

. . . Boards of education, presidents of colleges, and faculty advisers are not excepted from the rule that protects students against unreasonable rules and regulations. This court recognizes that the establishment of an educational program requires certain rules and regulations necessary for maintaining an orderly program and operating the institution in a manner conducive to learning. However, the school and school officials have always been bound by the requirement that the rules and regulations must be reasonable. Courts may only consider whether rules and regulations that are imposed by school authorities are a reasonable exercise of the power and discretion vested in those authorities. Regulations and rules which are necessary in maintaining order and discipline are always considered reasonable. In the case now before this court, it is clear that the maintenance of order and discipline of the students attending Troy State College had nothing to do with the rule that was invoked against Dickey. As a matter of fact, the president of the institution, President Adams, testified that his general policy of not criticizing the Governor or the State Legislature under any circumstances, regardless of how reasonable or justified the criticism might be, was not for the purpose of maintaining order and discipline among the students. On this point, President Adams testified that the reason for the rule was that a newspaper could not criticize its owners, and in the case of a state institution the owners were to be considered as the governor and the members of the legislature. . . .

With these basic constitutional principles in mind, the conclusion is compelled that the invocation of such a rule against Gary Clinton Dickey that resulted in his expulsion and/or suspension from Troy State College was unreasonable. A state cannot force a college student to forfeit his constitu-

28

tionally protected right of freedom of expression as a condition to his attending a state-supported institution. State school officials cannot infringe on their students' right of free and unrestricted expression as guaranteed by the Constitution of the United States where the exercise of such right does not "materially and substantially interfere with requirements of appropriate discipline in the operation of the school." . . . The defendants in this case cannot punish Gary Clinton Dickey for his exercise of this constitutionally guaranteed right by cloaking his expulsion or suspension in the robe of "insubordination." The attempt to characterize Dickey's conduct, and the basis for their action in expelling him, as "insubordination" requiring rather severe disciplinary action does not disguise the basic fact that Dickey was expelled from Troy State College for exercising his constitutionally guaranteed right of academic and/or political expression.

The court then explained that the college had made a mistake in firing the plaintiff as a student rather than as an editor. "There was," the court said, "no legal obligation on the school authorities to permit [him] to continue as one of the editors. As a matter of fact, there was no legal obligation . . . to operate a school paper."

Finally, looking to the aftermath of plaintiff's reinstatement the court had this observation to make:

Defendants' argument that Dickey's readmission will jeopardize the discipline in the institution is superficial and completely ignores the greater damage to college students that will result from the imposition of intellectual restraints such as the "Adams Rule" in this case. The imposition of such a restraint as here sought to be imposed upon Dickey and the other students at Troy State College violates the basic principles of academic and political expression as guaranteed by our Constitution.

The objectionable material in the Dickey case concerned

29

politics. In Antonelli v. Hammond[18] it concerned obscenity. Although in this case the court again upheld the student editor, the circumstances are sufficiently different to justify inclusion, particularly at a time when moral and aesthetic standards are in transition. The editor of the Fitchburg State campus newspaper, *The Cycle*, reprinted an article of Eldridge Cleaver's, "Black Moochie," which originally appeared in *Ramparts Magazine*. On grounds of obscenity the president of the college took exception to both the theme of the article and its use of four-letter words. To enforce his view he withheld vital funds from the student activities budget for the publication of the paper. The student sought to prohibit this action.

In order to assure some campus publication until the case came up in court, the editor agreed to cooperate with a faculty board of two appointed by defendant. The approval of this board was to be gained before the publication of each issue. No guidelines of what would be acceptable were laid down and no procedure designated whereby their reasonableness might be reviewed. Shortly after this compromise was set up the editor resigned because of a financial dispute with the board. No disciplinary action at any time was taken against the plaintiff as in the Dickey case and at all times he seemed to have the backing of the student body which elected him. As a result it seemed that the case might no longer need to be heard since the student lacked a legal interest in the outcome. The court held, however, that he had a continuing interest in spite of his resignation. "There is and there ought to be no rule of constitutional standing," the court said, "that in order to construct a justiciable 'case' a plaintiff must submit to the very burden whose validity he wishes to attack."

Since prerequisite review by the faculty board was a threat of previous restraint on freedom of expression, the court was skeptical of its constitutional validity. Exemptions from constitutional immunity to prior restraint, it said, are the exceptions rather than the rule. Continuing, the court made its position clear:

[18] 308 Fed. Supp. 1329 (1970).

Students

It is true that the advisory board proposes to suppress only obscene writings and that obscenity does not fall within the area of constitutionally protected speech or press. . . . However, the manner and means of achieving the proposed suppression are of crucial importance. . . . Whenever the state takes any measure to regulate obscenity it must conform to procedures calculated to avoid the danger that protected expression will be caught in the regulatory dragnet. . . .

The type of procedural safeguards required by the First Amendment was indicated [by] . . . the Supreme Court, [which] listed three minimal requirements: first, that the censor bear the burden of [proving obscenity]; second, that the requirement of advance submission not be so administered as to [preclude appeal]; and, third, that the procedure . . . assure a prompt . . . judicial determination.

Nothing of the sort is included in the system devised by the defendant. . . . The advisory board bears no burden other than exercising its judgment; there is no appeal within the system. . . . Indeed, final responsibility rests with two faculty members . . . [who] are wholly unfamiliar with the complex tests of obscenity established by the Supreme Court. . . . Accordingly, the court concludes that the defendant's establishment of the advisory board is . . . an unconstitutional exercise of state power. . . .

Free speech does not mean wholly unrestricted speech and the constitutional rights of students may be modified by regulations reasonably designed to adjust these rights to the needs of the school environment. The exercise of rights by individuals must yield when they are incompatible with the school's obligation to maintain the order and discipline necessary for the success of the educational process. . . .

No such justification has been shown. . . . Obscenity in a campus newspaper is not . . . apt to be significantly disruptive of an orderly and disciplined educational process. . . . The university setting of . . . students being exposed to a wide range of intellectual experience creates a relatively ma-

31

ture marketplace for the interchange of ideas so that the free speech clause of the First Amendment, with its underlying assumption that there is positive social value in an open forum, seems particularly appropriate. . . .

We are well beyond the belief that any manner of state regulation is permissible simply because it involves an activity which is a part of the university structure and is financed with funds controlled by the administration. The state is not . . . the unrestrained master of what it creates and fosters. Thus in cases concerning school-supported publications or the use of school facilities, the courts have refused to recognize as permissible any regulations infringing free speech when not shown to be . . . related to the maintenance of order and discipline. . . .

These decisions do not stand for the proposition that a state college administration has no more control over the campus newspaper than it would have over a private publication disseminated on campus. In the very creation of an activity involving media of communication, the state regulates to some degree the form of expression fostered. But the creation of the form does not give birth also to the power to mold its substance. . . .

Because of the potentially great social value of a free student voice in an age of student awareness and unrest it would be inconsistent with basic assumptions of First Amendment freedoms to permit a campus newspaper to be simply a vehicle for ideas the state or the college administration deems appropriate. Power to prescribe classroom curricula in state universities may not be transferred to areas not designed to be part of the curriculum.

In State v. Buchanan[19] quite a different issue of student freedom was involved. A coed wrote an article for the student newspaper on student use of marijuana on the university campus. At the same time a grand jury was investigating the use of this drug

[19] 436 P. 2nd 729 (1968).

in the community. The jury asked the defendant to disclose the sources of her information, which she refused to do on grounds that the information had been given her confidentially and she had promised her interviewees anonymity. She was held in contempt of court and appealed that judgment. Her argument was that the constitutional protection of freedom of the press extends to freedom to gather news. Since news stories like hers could not be obtained without the privilege of confidence, the order for her to divulge her sources abridged a protected freedom. In balancing a free press against the detection of law violators, she insisted the balance should be struck in favor of freedom of the press. The court, however, struck the balance the other way, holding that "the rights of privacy, freedom of association, and ethical convictions are subordinate to the duty of every citizen to testify in court." In a note concerning its decision the court pointed out that the legal privilege accorded at common law to communications of lawyers, clergymen, and physicians was attached to the communication and not to the identity of the privileged party. Although the court was unwilling to include news-gathering in the category of privileged communications, it did acknowledge the fact that a dozen or more states had passed statutes protecting news gatherers. As an incidental remark, the court opined that it saw nothing unconstitutional about such statutes.

A third unusual case involving student publications is that of Arvin v. Rutgers State University.[20] In this instance a student submitted to the *Rutgers Law Review* a manuscript criticizing the Civil Rights Act of 1875. From his analysis the student concluded that the United States Supreme Court had erred in its famous desegregation case of Brown v. Board of Education of Topeka. The student editor rejected the manuscript on the ground that a critique of the nineteenth century act from the angle of history alone was not enough. The writer's immediate reaction was that his article had been rejected because of its political conservatism rather than any scholarly deficiencies. The judge found that the writer had not been deprived of any federally protected right. "Freedom of speech," he declared, "is guaranteed by the Constitution, but the right to

[20] 385 Fed. 2nd 151 (1967).

33

have others listen is not guaranteed, nor is anyone obligated to read articles that an author is able to publish. It could not be contended reasonably that the editorial board of *Rutgers Law Review* must accept for publication every treatise on law which is submitted to it. There must necessarily be a broad area for the exercise of discretion."

Aligning itself with this opinion the appellate court further elaborated:

> *The right to freedom of speech does not open every avenue to one who desires to use a particular outlet for expression. . . . Nor does freedom of speech comprehend the right to speak on any subject at any time. . . . "True, if a man is to speak or preach he must have some place from which to do it. This does not mean, however, that he may seize a particular radio station for his forum." . . .*
>
> *One who claims that his constitutional right to freedom of speech has been abridged must show that he has a right to use the particular medium through which he seeks to speak. This the plaintiff has . . . failed to do. . . . [H]e may freely at his own expense print his article and distribute it to all who wish to read it. However, he does not have the right . . . constitutional or otherwise, to commandeer the press and columns of the* Rutgers Law Review *for the publication of his article, at the expense of the subscribers to the review and the New Jersey taxpayers, to the exclusion of other articles deemed by the editors to be more suitable for publication. On the contrary, the acceptance or rejection of articles submitted for publication in a law school law review necessarily involves the exercise of editorial judgment and this is in no wise lessened by the fact that the law review is supported, at least in part, by the state.*
>
> *The plaintiff's contention that the student editors of the* Rutgers Law Review *have been so indoctrinated in a liberal ideology by the faculty of the law school as to be unable to evaluate his article objectively is so frivolous as to require no discussion.*

Students

Military Service

Never has military service been so loathsome to students in the United States as during the involvement in the Vietnam War. Most recently students have manifested their hostility by trying to drive ROTC courses out of the curriculum. In some instances faculties have even joined them, masking their hostility by asserting that military courses have no academic merit. For a longer time, however, students have protested military service because of conscientious objection to war. Some have sought haven in foreign countries while others have had recourse to the courts. A leading case is that of Hanauer v. Elkins.[21] Plaintiffs were both students at the University of Maryland, a land grant institution receiving funds under the Morrill Act, which requires military instruction as part of the curriculum. Both sought to compel the university to admit them without exacting this requirement. They sought exemption because they found killing other human beings repugnant to their religious principles. There was no question of their sincerity even though the respective churches to which they belonged did not require them to be conscientious objectors. Both already had given two years of civilian service after being inducted under the Selective Service Act and had received certificates of discharge as draftees. One plaintiff admitted he might have gone to a private institution where military instruction was not required, but that would have been more expensive than attendance at a public institution like the University of Maryland. Besides, Maryland offered a special course which he wanted.

There were three strings to the bow of their argument. First, they contended that prescribed military courses were contrary to the charter of the university and the constitution of the state. From the charter they cited a provision that no sectarian or partisan test would be allowed in the admission of students, and another provision that the university would be maintained for students of every religious denomination without requiring any religious or civil test. From the state declaration of rights they cited that all persons were

[21] 217 Md. 213–141 A. 2nd 903 (1958).

35

equally entitled to protection in their religious liberty and that no law could molest a person on account of his religious beliefs. To this line of argument the court responded:

> *The university, in requiring the basic course as a part of the curriculum, is not imposing a religious test. . . . The question is . . . simply whether the policy of the university must yield to the views of the petitioners that the prescribed course is at variance with their . . . pacifist beliefs. The test of eligibility to attend the university is not directed at these petitioners. They are asserting a right to attend the university without compliance with a general condition which they are unwilling to meet because of religious convictions personal to them. We think the regulations adopted by the board of regents are well within any limitations imposed by the constitution and laws of this state.*

Second, the students sought the protection of the First and Fourteenth Amendments of the Federal Constitution. Here, too, the court found no invasion of their rights. Citing the earlier conscientious objector's case of Hamilton v. Regents of University of California,[22] the Maryland court quoted the concurring opinion of Justice Benjamin Cardozo (with whom, incidentally, Justices Louis Brandeis and Harlan Stone concurred):

> *The First Amendment, if it be read into the Fourteenth, makes invalid any state law "respecting an establishment of religion or prohibiting the free exercise thereof." Instruction in military science is not instruction in the practice or tenets of a religion. Neither directly nor indirectly is government establishing a state religion when it insists upon such training. Instruction in military science, unaccompanied here by any pledge of military service, is not an interference by the state with the free exercise of religion when the liberties of the Constitution are read in the light of a century and a half of history during days of peace and war. . . . The conscientious*

[22] 293 U.S. 245 (1935).

objector, if his liberties were to be thus extended, might refuse to contribute taxes in furtherance of a war, whether for attack or defense, or in furtherance of any other end condemned by his conscience as irreligious or immoral. The right of private judgment has never yet been so exalted above the powers and the compulsion of the agencies of government.

Third, the students argued that since they had already performed their civilian service under the Selective Service Act, they should be exempted from further exposure to the military. "But we," responded the Maryland court, "think the answer is that the act of Congress according the exemption was a matter of grace, not conferring any federal right that would [force] this state . . . to accord an equivalent exemption. . . . If we assume . . . that Congress has any Constitutional power to supersede the state policy in the training of its youth, it is sufficient to say that Congress has not yet attempted to do so."

At one point in their argument that military service had religious overtones, the students cited the well known case of West Virginia State Board of Education v. Barnette,[23] in which a state law requiring the hand salute to the flag in school was declared unconstitutional. But the Maryland court distinguished the Hanauer case on the grounds that school attendance was compulsory in the Barnette case, and that the hand salute was a form of utterance compelling students to declare a belief.

Domicile

For years out-of-state students have been at odds with the states in which they have been studying over two issues—whether they can vote where they study and, if they are attending a state-supported institution, whether they have to pay in-state or out-of-state tuition. The problem is the same in both instances, distinguishing where the student resides from where he is domiciled. The issue may seem one of semantics, but it refers to a real and significant difference. Petitioners in Matter of Robbins v. Chamberlain[24] were

[23] 319 U.S. 626 (1942).
[24] 297 N.Y. 108–75 N.E. 2nd 617 (1947).

The Courts and Higher Education

Second World War veterans living in Shanks Village, which was formerly part of Camp Shanks and which had been put under the control of Columbia University by the Federal Public Housing Administration to be leased only to students. Petitioners had moved there with their families and were dividing their time between part-time work and studies. In spite of these circumstances their right to vote in Rockland County had been successfully contested by the election districts. The petitioners appealed the ruling.

The response of the court was:

> *Our Constitution and our statutes, for sufficient reasons, have decreed that those who attend colleges and seminaries away from their family homes and live in college residential halls during the college year in the fashion conventional before the war do not . . . become qualified to vote in the communities in whose life and doings these students [have] so limited a part and so limited an interest. The mischief against which the law was aimed was "the participation of an unconcerned body of men in the control through the ballot-box of municipal affairs in whose further conduct they have no interest, and from the mismanagement of which by the officers their ballots might elect, they sustain no injury." . . . However, that old concept of semicloistered college life has little to do with the way these petitioners are getting their education. They are married men who have left their parental firesides and gone out on their own with their wives and children. Their living arrangements at Shanks Village bear small resemblance to an old-fashioned college community, but are more like the kind of new-fashioned company-owned housing projects, which great industries build near their factories to attract and serve their employees and their employees' families. These students are family men, not college boys away from their parental homes. True, their tenure of occupancy at Shanks Village can continue only while they are students, but since they have no other homes their tenure is "temporary" or "indefinite" only in*

38

the same sense as the tenure of the occupant of a city apartment house.

There is no substantial dispute of fact here. These petitioners have shown their eligibility to vote from the only residences they have. As to the right to vote of the petitioners who are wives or parents of veteran-students, we cannot see that there is any doubt whatever.

In deciding this case the court was apparently trying to highlight the importance of intent. Is the intent of the petitioners to be transient or to be settled? Many courts use residence to refer to where one is currently living and domicile to refer to where one intends to return or abide, thus making a distinction by which most students are merely residents because their domiciles are with their parents. Petitioners, however, not only were residents in Rockland County but were domiciled there as well, and the court saw no intent of transience.

Dormitories

Now that students are seeking to make their own rules for the dormitories in which they live and when the university no longer seems to represent a parent to them, the following two cases may be minor landmarks. In Moore v. Student Affairs Committee of Troy State University[25] the plaintiff's name was on a list of students suspected of possession of marijuana. Late one morning the list was presented by federal agents to the dean of men at the university for permission to search the rooms. The list had been drawn up on the basis of information from reliable sources. In the early afternoon of the same day the agents received further information that some of the students named were packing to leave the campus for a break, and fearing that their quarry might escape, the agents and the dean searched the plaintiff's room without a warrant and without his consent. The search turned up a quantity of marijuana, and as a result plaintiff was indefinitely suspended. He sought reinstatement

[25] 284 Fed. Supp. 725 (1968).

primarily because his Fourth Amendment freedom from unreasonable search and seizure had been invaded and therefore the marijuana should not have been permitted as evidence.

The college quoted a leaflet on residence hall policies which stated that the college reserved the right to enter rooms for inspection purposes and that if the administration deemed it necessary the room might be searched. The court declared:

> *College students who reside in dormitories have a special relationship with the college involved. Insofar as the Fourth Amendment affects that relationship, it does not depend on either a general theory of the right of privacy or on traditional property concepts. The college does not stand, strictly speaking,* in loco parentis *to its students nor is their relationship purely contractual in the traditional sense. The relationship grows out of the peculiar and sometimes . . . competing interests of college and student. A student naturally has the right to be free of unreasonable search and seizures, and a tax-supported public college may not compel a "waiver" of that right as a condition [for] admission. The college, on the other hand, has an . . . obligation . . . to enforce reasonable regulations designed to protect campus order and discipline and to promote an environment consistent with the educational process. The validity of the regulation authorizing search of dormitories thus does not depend on whether a student "waives" his right to Fourth Amendment protection [but rather] . . . is determined by whether the regulation is a reasonable exercise of the college's supervisory duty. . . .*
>
> *The student is subject only to reasonable rules and regulations, but his rights must yield to the extent that they would interfere with the institution's fundamental duty to operate the school as an educational institution. A reasonable right of inspection is necessary to the institution's performance of that duty even though it may infringe on the outer boundaries of a dormitory student's Fourth Amendment rights. . . . The regulation of Troy State University in issue here is thus facially reasonable. . . .*

The regulation was reasonably applied in this case. The constitutional boundary line between the right of the school authorities to search and the right of a dormitory student to privacy must be based on a reasonable belief on the part of the college authorities that a student is using a dormitory room for a purpose which is illegal or which would otherwise seriously interfere with campus discipline. Upon this submission, it is clear that such a belief existed in this case. . . .

[The] standard of "reasonable cause to believe" to justify a search by college administrators—even where the sole purpose is to seek evidence of suspected violations of law—is lower than the constitutionally protected criminal law standard of "probable cause." This is true because of the special necessities of the student-college relationship and because college disciplinary proceedings are not criminal proceedings in the constitutional sense. It is clearly settled that due process in college disciplinary proceedings does not require . . . hearings subject to rules of evidence and all constitutional criminal guaranties.

The issue of dormitory control was quite different in Jones v. Vassar.[26] For years Vassar had been a college strictly for women, but in the trend toward coeducation the college yielded to the new policy. With men on the Vassar campus the issue of visiting hours for men in women's dormitories presented itself, and the students elected unrestricted hours. However, the mother of one of the girls claimed that the college had a duty to her and other parents to maintain the old dormitory rules and that allowing the students to make this drastic change amounted to a breach of contract. The court thought otherwise:

In academic communities greater freedoms may prevail than in society at large and the subtle fixing of these limits should, to a great degree, be left to the educational institution itself. . . . The judiciary must exercise restraint in question-

[26] 299 N.Y.S. 283 (1969).

ing the wisdom of specific rules or the manner of their application, since such matters are ordinarily in the prerogative of school administrators rather than the courts.

There has been no showing by plaintiff that there was an abuse of discretion by defendants in . . . adopting the new . . . regulations and this court will not interfere with defendant's discretion.

The plaintiffs urge that the court should interfere to protect alleged invasions of the students' right of privacy by forbidding unlimited visiting hours for males; however, as a matter of law, the plaintiffs are not entitled to an injunction since the complaint and other affidavits do not show that the plaintiffs have suffered or will suffer immediate and irreparable damage. Mere speculation as to the possible consequences of conduct complained of in the complaint is insufficient. . . .

Private colleges and universities are governed on the principle of academic self-regulation, free from judicial restraints. . . . Vassar College, like other previously all female institutions, has succumbed to the trend of coeducation and with the advent of males, new difficulties will be encountered by the college administration. It is the privilege of a college, through its Student Government Association, to promulgate and enforce rules and regulations for the social conduct of students without judicial interference.

The court thought its decision was required not only by the traditional principle of academic self-regulation but also by that subcategory of academic self-regulation, academic freedom. In the United States academic freedom generally refers to the freedom of the professor to express diverse opinions in teaching, and therefore seems inapplicable to the Vassar case. The Germans, however, have made a distinction in academic freedom to include the freedom of the student to arrange his academic life. If one accepts this distinction, academic freedom becomes relevant.

Societies

American students long have organized on campus to provide themselves with activities not found in the curriculum. As these activities arose independently of the regular studies, they have occasionally presented problems when they were not in line with official campus policies. Consequently the trend has been for college and university authorities to extend control over these organizations. An interesting challenge to this growing control occurred in Eisen v. Regents of University of California.[27] In this case the plaintiff was an officer in a student organization which was engaged in advocating dissident ideas but which had qualified to be registered at the university. One condition of registration was that the organization had to submit a statement of its purposes and a roll of its officers; the regents had a policy that this information was freely available to the public. The plaintiff student sought to restrain the regents from disclosing his name on the ground that disclosure would be a deterrent to the exercise of his constitutional rights of free speech and assembly. Neither he nor the university was at issue over the principle that "ideas, no matter how unpopular or erroneous in their dissemination, including the formation of groups and associations to advance such ideas, are fully protected by the First Amendment."

Weighing the social interests involved here, the court sided with the defendant.

> *Just as the people of the state have a right to know how their elected officials conduct the public business, they are entitled to know the identity [of] responsible officers of organizations that are granted the privileges of becoming campus organizations and using the public property and facilities of the university. [It cannot] be successfully argued that the protection of plaintiff's First Amendment rights requires complete anonymity. The U.S. Supreme Court has held that First Amendment freedoms are not violated by legislation requiring "a modicum of information." . . .*
>
> *Nor . . . can it be said that the identification requirement of the university's policy and the disclosure of this lim-*

---

[27] 75 Cal. Reptr. 45 (1969). (California in the past decade or so has become an exception to the footnote style detailed in footnote one in this chapter.)

*ited information to a member of the public would unduly de-
ter the freedom of expression of dissident organizations and
their officers. . . .*

> *Impairments of First Amendment rights are balanced
by determining whether there is a reasonable relationship between the impairment and a subject of overriding and compelling state interest. . . . There can be no doubt that disclosure requirements may impair rights of free speech and
association and that First Amendment rights are primarily intended to protect minority views. . . . We conclude, however,
. . . that here the compelling interest of the public in being
able to ascertain the information contained in the registration
statement outweighs any minimal infringement of plaintiff's
First Amendment rights.*

The courts have gone much further regarding the control
of student societies than they did in the Eisen case. A notable pocket
of resistance to this control has been Greek letter societies with national affiliates whose policies are at odds with local academic
administrations, especially in situations where the academic administration has outlawed racial discrimination. Webb v. State University of New York[28] is perhaps the most emphatic assertion of university control on record. Shortly after the university was established
its board of trustees passed resolutions stating that no social organization affiliated with any national or other organization would be
permitted at the university and that no social organization, in policy
or practice, could bar students on account of race, color, religion,
creed, national origin, or other artifical criteria. The university president was authorized to determine which student organizations were
social as distinguished from those which were scholastic or religious.

Members and affiliates of national fraternities sought to void
these resolutions on the grounds that they infringed their civil rights
to freedom of assembly, to equal protection of the laws, and to notice and hearing. They also introduced evidence to show the positive
benefits from national affiliation. But Judge Augustus Hand, speaking for the Federal Circuit Court, countered:

[28] 125 Fed. Supp. 910 (1954).

44

Students

The constitutionality of the action taken here cannot be questioned. A state may adopt such measures, including the outlawing of certain social organizations, as it deems necessary to its duty of supervision and control of its educational institutions. . . . Moreover, the incidental effect of any . . . policy . . . upon individuals or organizations outside the university is not a basis for attack. . . .

Plaintiffs argue that they were not notified of the pending action, but lack of notice and hearing before adoption of a resolution by an administrative body is not a denial of due process where legislative action of a prospective nature is taken under a valid delegation of powers from the legislature.

TWO

Faculty

Appointment and Resignation

Recruiting new faculty is ordinarily undertaken by heads of departments or deans of schools or both. Although chairmen or deans are the apparent agents of a college, the prospective recruit should be on his guard that the legal realities may not be what they seem, as is well illustrated in Sittler v. Board of Control.[1] In a telephone conversation the chairman of the German department engaged plaintiff on a one year appointment. Subsequently he wrote plaintiff a letter confirming the telephone conversation and stating further details of the position both financial and academic. After he had taught for two months, plaintiff's contract was abruptly terminated and he initiated a suit to recover damages. Defendant claimed that the head of the German department had no authority to make a contract, such authority being reserved by statute for the school's governing board. The court also challenged plaintiff's interpretation of the arrangements.

> *Plaintiff asserts that the power to contract with teachers may be delegated, and in the instant case that it is at least a question of fact if such power were not delegated by the board of control to Professor Bennett. . . . But the instant case involves the right by contract to bind*

[1] 333 Mich. 681—53 N.E. 2nd 681 (1952).

46

the state in the operation of one of its educational institutions over a period of time and to expend public funds. . . . Powers of the character vested by . . . statutory provisions in a board of control of an educational institution maintained by the state cannot be delegated to some subordinate or representative.

It follows that plaintiff did not possess a contract under which he could assert rights. Even the letter written by Professor Bennett does not purport on its face to be a contract. We are mindful that it appears . . . that on other occasions heads of departments have hired assistant teachers, but such usage or custom, if it ever prevailed, cannot be availed of to enlarge the statutory powers of the board of control so as to include or justify acts which are unauthorized.

Interestingly enough the same rule holds for resignations. In State Normal School v. Wightman[2] a professor tendered his resignation to the college president and shortly thereafter sent its revocation to the board of trustees before the president had acted on it. Did the resignation take effect or not? Part of the professor's salary hung on this issue. The outcome turned on who was authorized to accept the resignation. The court decided:

A contract of employment becomes effective when the appointee has accepted. So also an offer by the appointee to terminate or surrender an appointment by resignation is effectual only when the resignation is duly accepted by the body whose duty it is to make or terminate the appointment. . . . The trustees alone have the power to accept a resignation and thus to sever the contractual relation between the college and a member of its faculty, even as they alone have the power to establish that relation. An effort was made by the trustees to show that they had given instructions to the president to employ and discharge members of the faculty, but the lower court properly ruled out all evidence of such unauthorized delegation of the trustees' statutory powers and duties.

[2] 93 Colo. 226—25 P. 2nd 193 (1933).

47

In the next case the issue was not over the authority to employ but whether that authority had been properly exercised. Kay v. Board of Higher Education[3] was a case in which the board engaged Bertrand Russell, the late English philosopher and mathematician, to teach mathematics at the City College of New York. Petitioner challenged the legality of the appointment. Three points were made against Russell—that he was not a United States citizen as required by New York State education law, that he had not taken a written qualifying examination as demanded by the civil service act, and that his private life and writings, especially as they revealed his unconventional views on sex, made him morally unfit to teach. It seems fair to say that the real issue in this case was neither that Russell was not a United States citizen nor that he had not submitted to a written test of his academic qualifications. If it were the former then no foreign savant could be invited to sharpen the minds of the city's youth. If it were the latter the question arises, who would be capable of examining one of the world's greatest logicians and mathematicians? The issue seems rather to have been whether Russell's ideas about unrelated matters (or if related, only tangentially or peripherally so) should bar him from the position he had been invited to occupy.

The judge thought they should, and sustained the petitioner on all three points. He based his opinion on what he thought contemptible in Russell's writings, saying, "The contention of the petitioner that Mr. Russell has taught in his books immoral and salacious doctrines is amply sustained by the books . . . which were offered in evidence. It is not necessary to detail here the filth which is contained in the books." The judge did not ignore the insidious impact of such convictions on Russell's teaching.

It has been argued that the private life and writings of Mr. Russell have nothing whatsoever to do with his appointment as a teacher. . . .

But there are certain basic principles upon which this government is founded. If a teacher who is a person not of

[3] 18 N.Y.S. 2nd 821 (1940).

good moral character is appointed by any authority, the appointment violates these essential prerequisites. One of the prerequisites of a teacher is good moral character. . . . It needs no argument here to defend this statement. It need not be found in the education law. It is found in the nature of the teaching profession. Teachers are supposed not only to impart instruction in the classroom but [also] by their example to teach the students.

Realizing that he was setting his judgment of Russell's fitness to teach against that of the City Board of Higher Education, the judge turned to this final facet of the case:

Conceding . . . that the board of higher education has sole and exclusive power to select the faculty of City College and that its discretion cannot be reviewed or curtailed by this court or any other agency, nevertheless such sole and exclusive power may not be used to . . . encourage any course of conduct tending to a violation of the Penal Law. . . . [H]is appointment violates a perfectly obvious canon of pedagogy, namely, that the personality of the teacher has more to do with forming a student's opinion than many syllogisms. A person we despise and who is lacking in ability cannot argue us into imitating him. A person whom we like and who is of outstanding ability does not have to try. It is contended that Bertrand Russell is extraordinary. That makes him the more dangerous. The philosophy of Mr. Russell and his conduct in the past is in direct conflict [with] and in violation of the penal law of the State of New York. When we consider how susceptible the human mind is to the ideas and philosophy of teaching professors, it is apparent that the board of higher education either disregarded the probable consequences of their acts or were more concerned with advocating a cause that appeared to them to present a challenge to so-called academic freedom without according suitable consideration [to] the other aspects of the problem. . . . While this court would not interfere with any action of the Board in so far as . . . valid academic freedom is concerned, it will not tolerate academic freedom being used as a cloak to promote the popularization in the minds of adolescents of acts forbidden by the penal law. This appointment affects the public health, safety and morals of the community and it is the duty of the court to act. Academic freedom does not mean academic license. It is the freedom to do good and not to teach evil. Academic freedom cannot authorize a teacher to teach that murder or treason are good.

Although the judge rested his opinion somewhat on his conception of academic freedom, the issue seems rather to have been one involving civil liberty. Ordinarily academic freedom pertains to opinions expressed within the scope of the professor's chair. Here the controversial matters were quite extraneous to Russell's proffered chair in logic and mathematics. His views on sex came rather within the scope of his civil liberties. In this area it seems that the Board of Higher Education was as competent to judge of Russell's moral fitness as the judge himself, if not more so. Indeed, it may be wondered whether the judge was justified in substituting his opinion on moral fitness in place of the board. It is most deplorable that this case was not taken to an appellate court where wider judicial talent could have been brought to bear.

Dismissal

Faculty have been dismissed from their academic posts for many reasons. Rules of tenure have been devised to protect faculty against the more arbitrary and capricious reasons, but tenure in turn has raised legal problems. In Worzella v. Board of Regents[4] a teacher was charged with insubordination and separated from the institution. The separation occurred without a statement of charges, notice, or hearing, all of which he was entitled to since he had tenure. The board countered that the tenure policy did not abrogate the constitutional and statutory rules under which it operated. By these rules it was authorized to employ and dismiss all . . . instruc-

[4] 77 So. Da. 447–93 N.W. 2nd 411 (1958).

50

tors in schools under its control and to delegate these powers provisionally to the president of any of these schools.

In interpreting these rules the court struck a serious blow at the theory and practice of tenure by announcing,

The exact meaning and intent of [the] so-called tenure policy eludes us. . . . We gather from it, in general, that a faculty member . . . cannot . . . be devested of tenure unless a complaint against him is filed by the president of the college. He is then entitled to have . . . a hearing before a tenure committee . . . [which then] makes its recommendations to the president. The president must then decide whether to recommend the dismissal of the accused faculty member to the board of regents. The faculty member whose dismissal is recommended may appeal for a hearing before the board. The concluding paragraph states that the tenure policy is based "upon good faith between the college administration and the individual faculty member."

The policy statement is silent as to the board of regents' authority. By inference we may assume the board would have power to discharge a faculty member having tenure [only] when recommended by the tenure committee and president. Otherwise the board would have no authority to act. Apparently the board could not discharge or remove a faculty member with tenure for any reason if the president failed or refused to recommend dismissal. We believe this to be an unlawful abdication of the board's exclusive prerogative and power. . . .

The . . . statutory provisions merely confirm and clarify the board of regents' constitutional power to employ and dismiss all officers, instructors, and employees at all institutions under its control. These provisions become a part of every contract of employment entered into by the board. . . . [This power] cannot be restricted, surrendered, or delegated away. Our constitution prescribes that our state university and colleges "shall be under the control" of the board of regents. Without the right to employ, and the power to discharge,

51

its employees the board loses its constitutional right of control. . . .

The board of regents "may delegate provisionally to the president, dean, principal, or faculty of any school under its control so much of the authority conferred by this section as in its judgment seems proper . . ." This is a limited power. It does not empower the board to delegate away all of its powers or its constitutional duty of control. Under its provisions the board may only delegate the limited authority conferred on it by the same section.[5]

The next two cases deal with failure to reappoint, an action tantamount to dismissal. The plaintiff in Raney v. Trustees of Coalinga Junior College[6] was in the second year of his probationary period when the board notified him that he would not be reappointed for a third year. On request the board served him with a specification of charges which stated that his severe philosophy, particularly with respect to grading, was unsuitable for the junior college level and caused excessive dropouts during the semester. His tough philosophy, his sarcasm towards his students, particularly those who disagreed with his philosophy, resulted in many students either failing to take his course or failing to complete it, resulting in students missing an important basic course. He had originally been employed as a counselor but had proved ineffective due to poor rapport with his students. In addition he had a general reputation among students, faculty, and the community as a contentious person, which lessened their respect for him, thereby reducing his effectiveness as a teacher. Plaintiff sought to compel his reemployment, but the trial court was of the opinion that there was substantial evidence before the board to sustain these findings and the consequent dismissal. An appellate court saw no reason to disturb this decision, saying,

[5] Clark Byse, a legal scholar who has made a special study of tenure cases, disagrees with this decision and is hopeful that when a similar case comes up a contrary result will be reached. See "Academic Freedom, Tenure, and the Law: A Comment on Worzella v. Board of Regents," 73 *Harvard Law Review* 304.

[6] 48 Cal. Reptr. 555 (1966).

Faculty

If this court were at liberty to supervise the judgment of the members of the school board and to reverse their decision as to the retention of appellant on the basis of his ability and merits as a teacher, we might well reach an opposite conclusion. As remarked by the learned trial judge, who had been both a teacher and a school trustee prior to his elevation to the bench, Mr. Raney ". . . is a highly intelligent [and] courageous . . . individual," and the record evidences qualities of the petitioner which are desirable in the profession. If education is to achieve its asserted end of causing young people to think and to reach independent conclusions about the issues that agitate the world, there must be afforded to their teachers a sufficient independence to permit them to inculcate these virtues. Ideally, a teacher should be a little contentious, rather than stodgy and lethargic, but our theory of government gives to the school trustees, for better or for worse, an almost absolute choice either to hire or fire teachers who have not yet attained tenure. It might well be argued that the legislature has created a mirage for probationary teachers by seeming to assure them that they may demand a hearing if they are not retained for a fourth year. In practice, such an official inquiry does not result in a reinstatement of the teacher but only produces a possibly expanded assignment of reasons why the board does not wish to give him permanent status by rehiring him for a fourth year. This is how it is, and probationary teachers should clearly understand the way of the world insofar as their jobs are concerned.

In a recent case, Jones v. Hopper,[7] the probationer claimed he had a right to "expect" continued employment. His employment would have been continued, he contended, if he had not exercised his civil rights in a manner offensive to defendant, primarily by opposing the Vietnam war due to religious convictions. Under the Civil Rights Act he claimed an infringement of these rights. The lower court dismissed the case because plaintiff had not made out

[7] 410 Fed. 2nd 1323 (1969).

53

a legal cause of action for his claim to an expectancy. The appellate court agreed with the lower one, stating:

> *The Supreme Court has consistently held . . . that government employment, in the absence of legislation, can be revoked at the will of the appointing officer. . . . The principle stated teaches that public employment may be denied altogether subject, however, to the restriction that unreasonable conditions may not be imposed upon the granting of public employment. There is nothing in the complaint to warrant an inference or conclusion that the Colorado statute nor its application herein went "beyond what might be justified in the exercise of the state's legitimate inquiry into the fitness and competency of its teachers." . . .*
>
> *Southern Colorado State College is a state academic institution organized and existing under Colorado law which vests the government and management of its affairs in a board of trustees, which has [the] . . . "power to appoint and remove all . . . professors." . . .*
>
> *We think this provision precludes Jones from having the relief he seeks in this proceeding. His claimed interest must find its source in his expired appointment which constituted whatever contract existed. The provision above acknowledged became a part of any contract that may have existed between him and the college.*
>
> *The provision specifically denies an expectancy to continued employment; therefore, absent an expectancy, there could be no interest. "One has no constitutional right to a 'remedy' against the lawful conduct of another."*
>
> *As demonstrated above the right, privilege, or immunity Jones alleges he was deprived of is nonexistent.*
>
> *Because of the special needs of the university, both public and private, great discretion must be given it in decisions about the renewal of contract during the probationary period. In deciding whether to rehire or grant tenure, the considerations involved go well beyond a judgment about general teaching competence.*

Faculty

It would be intolerable for the courts to . . . require an educational institution to hire or to maintain on its staff a professor or instructor whom it deemed undesirable and did not wish to employ. For the courts to impose such a requirement would be an interference with the operation of institutions of higher learning contrary to established principles of law and to the best traditions of education.

The decision was close, however, since two judges dissented. They took exception to the fact that the majority ruled out plaintiff's "expectancy" on purely legal grounds. According to them this expectancy might have been proved as a fact if the judge in the lower court had permitted the case to go to trial.

Conflict of Interest

In a day when there is much discussion of conflict of interest in public employment, it may be well to examine several facets of the problem in the context of higher education. In Jones v. Board of Control[8] the plaintiff, while teaching on the Board's faculty of law, filed papers with the Florida Secretary of State indicating an intent to run for the office of circuit judge. Prohibiting such a dual activity was a rule clearly stated in the board's faculty handbook, to which the professor's contract made a specific reference. Although the board informed him that the filing would be considered a breach of contract he was not deterred. The board terminated the contract and he sued for reinstatement. Plaintiff maintained that the rule unreasonably interfered with his right to seek work for which he was trained, but the court upheld the rule. It might have done so, it said, based on Justice Oliver Wendell Holmes' famous remark, "The petitioner [a policeman] may have a constitutional right to talk politics, but he has no constitutional right to be a policeman." It preferred, however, to rest its conclusion on the broader ground that:

The rule prohibits no one from teaching. Neither does it prohibit a teacher from running for public office. It merely

8 131 Fla. 713—131 S. 2nd 713 (1961).

55

provides that he cannot do both simultaneously. There is adequate justification for the rule in the public interest as well as in the interest of the university student body. . . . The demands upon the time and energies incident to a warmly contested campaign for an important public office would necessarily affect the efficiency of the candidate; the potential effect upon the students, not only as the result of such inefficiency, but also in the nature of the political influences that might be brought to bear upon them would be further justification; the potential involvement of the state university which is dependent upon public support from all political elements would be another major consideration supporting the reasonableness of the rule. Although appellant suggests that he might well have conducted his campaign in the evening so as not to interfere with his professorial duties, the reasons which we have epitomized above would still apply. Moreover, anyone who has ever been associated with a heated political campaign well knows that it involves handshaking, speech making, telephone calling, letter writing, and door to door campaigning from morning well into the night. To anyone familiar with the practical aspects of American politics, it is asking too much to expect him to agree that success in a strenuous political campaign can be achieved merely by appearances at Saturday afternoon fish fries or early evening precinct rallies. The result simply is that it would be extremely difficult for a university professor to conduct his classroom courses with efficiency over a period of eight to ten weeks while simultaneously beating the bushes in search of votes to elevate him to the position of a circuit judge.

The conflict of interest in Colorado School of Mines v. Neighbors[9] came from the direction of defendant's pocketbook. While serving as director of physical education he employed his off-hours as manager of a hotel cocktail lounge. The college notified him that if he wanted to continue in its employ he would have to

[9] 119 Colo. 399—203 P. 2nd 904 (1949).

forego this extra employment. He refused, maintaining that in no way had he been remiss in fulfilling his contract of employment with the college. His contract was terminated, and in a suit complicated by other factors the director counterclaimed for damages suffered in breach of contract. "None will say," declared the court, "that moral justification did not attend the action of the trustees in the premises."

But did legality attend? The school had the power to exclude Neighbors from the service contemplated in the contract, . . . but does it follow that its formal order of dismissal worked legal termination of its contractual obligation to pay salary for the term? . . . We think not. . . . Considering . . . that the contract of employment involved here contained no provision in relation to how Neighbors should employ his [spare time], . . . plus the fact that in relation to the discharge of his duties under the contract there was no complaint, we think that in the sense of its liability for salary as contracted, the school breached its obligation.

Academic Freedom

Although our Constitutional fathers early recognized the inestimable importance of free speech by incorporating it in the First Amendment, it is only comparatively recently—since the Second World War, as a matter of fact—that the courts have taken active cognizance of academic freedom as an indispensable dimension of First Amendment rights. Up to this time courts were wary about injecting themselves into the internal affairs of colleges and universities, but after the Second World War they began to see that academic freedom is not just an internal affair of the school but that its significance extends far beyond the campus to the intelligent conduct of social affairs in general. Increasingly aware of the critical stake that society has in the free pursuit of the truth, the courts have recently outdone themselves in hedging it with Constitutional guarantees. Although academic freedom has many facets, only four can be presented here.

The landmark case making academic freedom a concern of

the courts was Sweezy v. New Hampshire.[10] The state legislature commissioned the attorney general to investigate subversive activities, and a member of the faculty of the University of New Hampshire was subpoenaed for questioning. Asked whether he was or had ever been a member of the communist party, he replied in the negative. But, asked such questions about his class room instruction as, "Did you tell the class socialism was inevitable?" "Did you advocate Marxism?" "Did you espouse dialectical materialism?" he refused to answer. When ordered by the court to respond, he still refused and was sentenced to jail for contempt of court. On appeal the New Hampshire court affirmed the action of the lower court. It recognized that the questions about what the professor said in class were an interference with his constitutional freedoms but justified the interference on the ground that it might be reasonable to believe that he was advocating the overthrow of the government by force. What made such a belief reasonable was the fact that the professor was a socialist having several affiliations with groups cited by the House Committee on Un-American Activities. In addition he was coeditor of an article stating that although violence is abhorrent, it is less to be deplored when used by the Soviets than by capitalist countries.

Whereas the state court struck the balance of individual and social interests in favor of society, the United States Supreme Court struck it the opposite way. Said Justice Felix Frankfurter,

When weighed against the grave harm resulting from governmental intrusion into the intellectual life of a university, such justification for compelling a witness to discuss the contents of his lecture appears grossly inadequate. Particularly is this so where the witness has sworn that neither in the lecture nor at any other time did he ever advocate overthrowing the Government by force and violence.

Progress in the natural sciences is not remotely confined to findings made in the laboratory. Insights into the mysteries

[10] 354 U.S. 234 (1957).

of nature are born of hypothesis and speculation. The more so is this true in the pursuit of understanding in the groping endeavors of what are called the social sciences, the concern of which is man and society. The problems that are the respective preoccupations of anthropology, economics, law, psychology, sociology, and related areas of scholarship are merely departmentalized dealing, by way of manageable division of analysis, with interpenetrating aspects of holistic perplexities. For society's good—if understanding be an essential need of society —inquiries into these problems, speculations about them, stimulation in others of reflection upon them, must be left as unfettered as possible. Political power must abstain from intrusion into this activity of freedom, pursued in the interest of wise government and the people's well-being, except for reasons that are exigent and obviously compelling.

Chief Justice Warren, speaking for the majority of the court, made an even more sweeping claim for protecting petitioner's academic freedom:

The essentiality of freedom in the community of American universities is almost self-evident. No one should underestimate the vital role in a democracy that is played by those who guide and train our youth. To impose any strait jacket upon the intellectual leaders in our colleges and universities would imperil the future of our Nation. No field of education is so thoroughly comprehended by man that new discoveries cannot yet be made. Particularly is that true in the social sciences, where few, if any, principles are accepted as absolutes. Scholarship cannot flourish in an atmosphere of suspicion and distrust. Teachers and students must always remain free to inquire, to study, and to evaluate, to gain new maturity and understanding; otherwise our civilization will stagnate and die.

It is noteworthy that students as well as faculty have laid claim to the protective cloak of academic freedom. An outstanding instance of such a student claim occurred in the Free Speech Movement on the Berkeley campus of the University of California, reported in Goldberg v. Regents of University of California.[11] The early phase of this movement was directed toward freedom to discuss social problems. Later the issue expanded to whether free speech included "filthy speech." Students, bearing placards with obscene four-letter words emblazoned on them, were arrested for violating criminal statutes on obscenity and were cited by the dean of the university for having offended university regulations. In the general catalogue, for instance, it was stated that "unbecoming behavior" would result in disciplinary action by the university authorities. A faculty committee including one nonvoting student was appointed to hear the charges against the students. The outcome was suspension, which the students challenged as unconstitutional.

The court began by clarifying the issue, pointing out to both parties that the question was not whether plaintiffs were guilty of obscenity but whether the defendant's disciplinary action had imposed unconstitutional conditions on their continued attendance at the university. Next the court pointed out to plaintiffs that they were not being disciplined for protesting on the campus but for the way in which they did it.

> *The qualification imposed was simply that plaintiffs refrain from repeatedly, loudly, and publicly using certain terms which, when so used, clearly infringed on the minimum standard of propriety and the accepted norm of public behavior of both the academic community and the broader social community. Plaintiffs' contention that the words were used only in the context of their demonstration is not borne out by the record which indicates that the terms were used repeatedly, and often out of context, or when used in context given undue emphasis. The conduct of plaintiffs thus amounted to coercion rather than persuasion.*

This clarification enabled the court to lay bare what it regarded as the major unarticulated premise of plaintiffs' case, namely, that

[11] 57 Cal. Reptr. 463 (1967).

*since their purpose was to protest, they had a consti-
tutional right to do so whenever, however, and wherever they
pleased. That concept of constitutional law was vigorously and
forthrightly rejected by the United States Supreme Court. . . .
These cases recognize that it is not enough for the plaintiffs to assert they are exercising a right to claim absolute immunity against any form of social control or discipline, for it
is well recognized that individual freedoms and group interests
can and do clash. . . . An individual cannot escape from social constraint merely by asserting that he is engaged in political talk or action.*

As for the restraints imposed by the university, the court
found them reasonable.

*[The University] has the power to formulate and en-
force rules of student conduct that are appropriate and necessary to the maintenance of order and propriety, considering
the accepted norms of social behavior in the community, where
such rules are reasonably necessary to further the university's
educational goals. . . .*

*Unquestionably, the achievement of the university's
educational goals would preclude regulations unduly restrict-
ing the freedom of students to express themselves. . . . "[A]
function of free speech under our system of government is to
invite dispute. It may indeed best serve its high purpose when
it induces a condition of unrest, creates dissatisfaction with
conditions as they are, or even stirs people to anger. Speech is
often provocative and challenging. It may strike at prejudices
and preconceptions and have profound unsettling effects as it
presses for acceptance of an idea." . . .*

*Historically, the academic community has been unique
in having its own standards, rewards and punishments. Its
members have been allowed to go about their business of
teaching and learning largely free of outside interference. To
compel such a community to recognize and enforce precisely
the same standards and penalties that prevail in the broader*

social community would serve neither the special needs and interests of the educational institutions, nor the ultimate advantages that society derives therefrom. Thus, in an academic community greater freedoms and greater restrictions may prevail than in society at large, and the subtle fixing of these limits should, in a large measure, be left to the educational institution itself.

While on the topic of free speech that offends propriety, it is appropriate to consider the case of Close v. Lederle,[12] in which an art exhibit was so avant-garde that its nudes gave offense to many of its viewers. The artist, a member of the faculty of fine arts at the University of Massachusetts, had accepted an offer by the head of his department to exhibit his works in the student union for three weeks. Controversy over the display became so heated that the defendant, without consulting the artist, discontinued the exhibit before the end of the agreed period. Through the court the artist sought a declaration that the removal of his pictures deprived him of his rights under the First Amendment. In doing so he did not claim that he had a right to hang his pictures anytime or anywhere in the university but, having been asked to hang them, he claimed he could not have the length of his exhibit arbitrarily cut short.

Ordinarily one thinks of academic freedom in connection with the liberal arts. But here the federal district court extended this principle to the fine arts as well, taking the position that the defendants had no right to censor the exhibit merely for an offensiveness that fell short of unlawful obscenity. Said the federal circuit court:

We disagree. We first consider the nature and quality of plaintiff's interest. Plaintiff makes the bald pronouncement, "Art is as fully protected by the Constitution as political or social speech." It is true that in the course of holding a motion picture entitled to First Amendment protection the court said . . . that moving pictures affect public attitudes in ways

[12] 303 Fed. Supp. 1110 (1969).

62

"ranging from direct espousal of a political or social doctrine to the subtle shaping of thought which characterizes all artistic expression." However, this statement in itself recognizes that there are degrees of speech.

There is no suggestion, unless in its cheap titles, that plaintiff's art was seeking to express political or social thought. . . . Even as to verbal communication the extent of the protection may depend upon the subject matter. . . . We consider plaintiff's constitutional interest minimal.

In this posture we turn to the question whether defendants have demonstrated a sufficient counterinterest to justify their action. The corridor was a passageway, regularly used by the public, including children. . . . The defendants were entitled to consider the primary use to which the corridor was put. . . . On the basis of the complaints received, and even without such, defendants were warranted in finding the exhibit inappropriate in that use. Where there was, in effect, a captive audience, defendants had a right to afford protection against "assault upon individual privacy." . . . Freedom of speech must recognize, at least within limits, freedom not to listen. . . .

So far we have considered academic freedom for residents of the campus. Dickson v. Sitterson[13] was a case where academic freedom was claimed for off-campus speakers. A student organization had requested the university to invite the speakers to come on campus and expound some unconventional views. The request was denied because the state legislature had passed a statute against inviting any speakers who were known communists, who advocated the overthrow of the government, or who had pleaded the Fifth Amendment, and the board of trustees of the state university were directed to incorporate this policy into their regulations. Plaintiffs, who clearly fell within the prohibited categories, went to court to enjoin giving effect to these regulations. In disposing of the injunction the judge said,

[13] 280 Fed. Supp. 486 (1968).

The Courts and Higher Education

This court is not blind to world affairs, and can understand and appreciate the vital concern of the people of the State of North Carolina over the unregulated appearance of dedicated members of the Communist Party on the campuses of its state-supported institutions. . . . Certainly the state is under no obligation to provide a sanctuary for the Communist Party, or a platform for propagandizing its creed. . . .

It is beyond question that boards of trustees of state-supported colleges and universities have every right to promulgate and enforce rules and regulations, consistent with constitutional principles, governing the appearance of all guest speakers. . . . No one has an absolute right to speak on a college or university campus, but once such institution opens its doors to visiting speakers it must do so under principles that are constitutionally valid.

We are also aware that when student groups have the privilege of inviting speakers, the pressure of considerations of audience appeal may impel them to so prefer sensationalism as to neglect academic responsibility. Such apparently motivated the plaintiff students during the spring of 1966. If the offering of the sensational becomes their primary objective the resulting program may not complement the educational purposes of the university. One does not acquire an understanding of important racial problems by listening successively to a Stokely Carmichael or an H. Rap Brown and an officer of the Ku Klux Klan. Countering a Herbert Aptheker with an official of the American Nazi Party may furnish excitement for young people, but it presents no rational alternatives and has but dubious value as an educational experience. University students should not be insulated from the ideas of extremists, but there is danger that the voices of reason, throughout the broad spectrum they cover, will remain unheard if the clamor of extremists is disproportionately amplified on university platforms. A more balanced program, unenslaved by sensationalism, but reaching it, too, would not be calculated to evoke legislative response. . . .

Faculty

Nevertheless, gauged by constitutional standards, our view is that the . . . regulations adopted by the board of trustees . . . pursuant to [state] statutes are facially unconstitutional because of vagueness. . . .

It is firmly established that a statute "which either forbids or requires the doing of an act in terms so vague that men of common intelligence must necessarily guess at its meaning and differ as to its application . . ." violates the due process clause of the Fourteenth Amendment because of vagueness. . . . Moreover, standards of permissible statutory vagueness are particularly strict when First Amendment rights are involved. . . .

The first provision of the statute under attack covers a "known member of the Communist Party." Known to whom, and to what degree of certainty? Known according to what standard? A member in what sense? Does it include membership in a communist front organization? Is it a matter of general reputation or rumor, or the personal knowledge of the chancellor? The statutes and regulations provide no clues to any of these questions. Without such answers, neither those who must obey nor those who must enforce the statutes and regulations can determine the extent of their obligation.

The next provision of the statute requires regulations covering visiting speakers who are "known to advocate the overthrow of the Constitution of the United States or the State of North Carolina." Does it mean with force and arms or is the advocacy of ideas sufficient? Must the advocacy be public or private? Is the advocacy of peaceful change included? It is sufficient to say that reasonable men might differ on the answers to these questions.

The third section of the statute covers speakers who have "pleaded the Fifth Amendment of the Constitution of the United States." Presumably, this means the self-incrimination clause, although this is a matter of conjecture. What is meant by "subversive connections"? Here again, since reasonable men might differ, the statute is unconstitutionally vague.

65

Moreover, the imposition of any sanction by reason of the invocation of the Fifth Amendment is constitutionally impermissible.

The final facet of academic freedom to be taken up here is the use of buildings for the discussion of controversial issues. In Matter of Buckley v. Meng[14] the defendant had an arrangement to lease plaintiff one of the auditoriums of Hunter College for a lecture series. So much controversy arose after a rightist meeting that the dean terminated the lease. In correspondence with plaintiff, Hunter's president stated that the college was not available for political groups to present a distinct position opposed by substantial parts of the public. The president added that the rationale of Hunter's policy was that academic institutions of a public character must avoid giving the appearance that they favor particular groups over other groups. The published policies governing use of the college facilities did specify some permissible nonacademic uses, but required that they be compatible with the aims and reputation of the college.

The judge was not impressed by these requirements.

> *In my view, the Hunter College regulations are either so vague as to invite discriminatory and arbitrary regulations, or else must be taken to rest upon a classification of uses which has no place in a democratic society because it stifles rather than stimulates the free discussion of vital public issues.*
>
> *Freedom of speech is "basic to a free and dynamic society." . . . It is in the light of the paramount value of free expression that the courts have drawn the corollary rule that any limitations on such expression must be drawn with precision. . . . We value speech so highly that we will only enforce a restriction on speech which is not subject to expansion at the discretionary whim of one who applies it. . . .*
>
> *In the first place, the regulation bespeaks its own indefiniteness by reason of the fact that it expressly provides that in order to qualify, a program must be "determined to be com-*

[14] 35 Misc. 2nd 467 (1962).

patible with the aims of Hunter College." Thus, a decision as to whether a program is permissible depends on a determination outside the scope and terms of the regulation. Who is empowered to make such a determination? And by what standards? In effect, whether a program is permissible or not rests on the untrammelled discretion of some official.

In the second place, even if we neglect this imperfection, and read the regulation as providing that "other programs" are permissible if they are "compatible with the aims of Hunter College," . . . we are left to bare speculation and surmise in deciding whether a use is permissible or not. . . .

I would have thought, for instance, that one of the aims of a college worthy of the name was to stimulate thought and to provoke intellectual controversy. The action of the dean of administration and the president of Hunter in this case bespeaks a contrary belief—they seem to regard intellectual quiescence and freedom from any conceivable identification with strongly expressed views as being necessary to their educational goals. I do not, of course, judicially deny them the right to determine the aims of their college. I do judicially hold, however, that consistency with the aims of the college is not a sufficiently clear standard by which to determine who shall use the college's facilities because reasonable men can and do differ as to what these aims are.

If I am correct in supposing that one of the criteria for the use of Hunter College's facilities is whether or not the proposed program presents a popular, noncontroversial point of view—one which is not "opposed by substantial parts of the public," to quote the president's words—it would follow that the standard for the use of the facilities is indeed clear. It would also follow, however, that this clear standard is itself unconstitutional because it discriminates against the expression of unpopular, minority opinion.

It should be stated at once that the college officials are not so crass as to reject minority viewpoints because of their content; they would prevent minorities of the right as well as of the left from expounding their views in the college halls. Their motives are rather to avoid identification with any minority position and to avoid picketing and other such "disturbances" . . . which sometimes attend . . . the public meetings of dissident groups. To my mind, as well-intentioned as these aims are, they evidence a temper of mind alien to the spirit of liberty and incompatible with the philosophy of the First Amendment.

Loyalty Oaths and Fifth Amendment

Academic freedom has been threatened indirectly as well as directly. Perhaps most menacing of the indirect attacks has been the exaction of loyalty oaths from professors. Under guise of protecting public security, state legislatures have harassed and intimidated teachers who have had the courage to be critical of the existing state of affairs and the temerity to suggest better ways of dealing with them. Oklahoma was one of the states that enacted a teacher-oath law. Among other features the Oklahoma oath required the teacher to affirm that within the five years immediately preceding the taking of the oath he had not been a member of any group which has been officially determined by the Attorney General or other authorized public agency to be a communist front or subversive organization. In Wieman v. Updegraff[15] the appellant had not taken this oath and the respondent had therefore sought to prohibit state officials from paying the teacher's salary at the Oklahoma Agricultural and Mechanical Arts College. Appellant countered by trying to compel payment of his salary regardless of whether he had taken the oath.

Threading its way through the argument the court said,

We are thus brought to the question . . . whether the Due Process Clause permits a state, in attempting to bar disloyal individuals from its employ, to exclude persons solely on the basis of organizational membership, regardless of their knowledge concerning the organizations to which they had be-

[15] 344 U.S. 183 (1952).

*longed. For, under the statute before us, the fact of member-
ship alone disqualifies. . . .*

*But membership may be innocent. A state servant may
have joined a proscribed organization unaware of its activities
and purposes. In recent years, many completely loyal persons
have severed organizational ties after learning . . . of the
character of groups to which they had belonged. . . . At the
time of affiliation, a group itself may be innocent, only later
coming under the influence of those who would turn it toward
illegitimate ends. Conversely, an organization formerly subversive and therefore designated as such may have subsequently
freed itself from the influences which originally led to its listing.*

*There can be no dispute about the consequences visited
upon a person excluded from public employment on disloyalty
grounds. In the view of the community, the stain is a deep
one; indeed, it has become a badge of infamy. Especially is
this so in time of cold war and hot emotions when "each man
begins to eye his neighbor as a possible enemy." Yet under the
Oklahoma Act, the fact of association alone determines disloyalty and disqualification; it matters not whether association
existed innocently or knowingly. To thus inhibit individual
freedom of movement is to stifle the flow of democratic expression and controversy at one of its chief sources. . . . In-
discriminate classification of innocent with knowing activity
must fall as an assertion of arbitrary power. The oath offends
due process.*

In a concurring opinion, Justice Hugo Black of the United
States Supreme Court went on to say:

*Test oaths are notorious tools of tyranny. When used
to shackle the mind they are, or at least they should be, un-
speakably odious to a free people. Test oaths are made still
more dangerous when combined with bills of attainder which
like this Oklahoma statute impose pains and penalties for past
lawful associations and utterances.*

Governments need and have ample power to punish

treasonable acts. But it does not follow that they must have a further power to punish thought and speech as distinguished from acts. Our own free society should never forget that laws which stigmatize and penalize thought and speech of the unorthodox have a way of reaching, ensnaring, and silencing many more people than at first intended. We must have freedom of speech for all or we will in the long run have it for none but the cringing and the craven. And I cannot too often repeat my belief that the right to speak on matters of public concern must be wholly free or eventually be wholly lost.

It seems self-evident that all speech criticizing government rulers and challenging current beliefs may be dangerous to the status quo. With full knowledge of this danger the framers rested our First Amendment on the premise that the slightest suppression of thought, speech, press, or public assembly is still more dangerous. This means that individuals are guaranteed an undiluted and unequivocal right to express themselves on questions of current public interest. It means that Americans discuss such questions as of right and not on sufferance of legislatures, courts or any other governmental agencies. It means that courts are without power to appraise and penalize utterances upon their notion that these utterances are dangerous. In my view this uncompromising interpretation of the Bill of Rights is the one that must prevail if its freedoms are to be saved. Tyrannical totalitarian governments cannot safely allow their people to speak with complete freedom. I believe with the framers that our free government can.

The danger that the oath will put the profession in an intellectual strait jacket is so menacing that the concurring opinion of Justice Felix Frankfurter is added for further reinforcement:

That our democracy ultimately rests on public opinion is a platitude of speech but not a commonplace in action. Public opinion is the ultimate reliance of our society only if it be disciplined and responsible. It can be disciplined and responsible only if habits of open-mindedness and of critical in-

quiry are acquired in the formative years of our citizens. The process of education has naturally enough been the basis of hope for the endurance of our democracy on the part of all our great leaders, from Thomas Jefferson onwards.

To regard teachers—in our entire educational system, from the primary grades to the university—as the priests of our democracy is therefore not to indulge in hyperbole. It is the special task of teachers to foster those habits of open-mindedness and critical inquiry which alone make for responsible citizens, who, in turn, make possible an enlightened and effective public opinion. Teachers must fulfill their function by precept and practice, by the very atmosphere which they generate; they must be exemplars of open-mindedness and free inquiry. They cannot carry out their noble task if the conditions for the practice of a responsible and critical mind are denied to them. They must have the freedom of responsible inquiry, by thought and action, into the meaning of social and economic ideas, into the checkered history of social and economic dogma.

The State of Washington also had a teacher-oath statute but it suffered from a different infirmity. The legislature required a loyalty oath, and in another act established that the state would not employ any subversive person. The case of Baggett v. Bullitt[16] arose when several dozen faculty and students of the University of Washington took legal action to restrain the university from enforcing these two acts. They took the stand that these acts were unconstitutionally vague and the United States Supreme Court agreed with them.

[In the] Washington statute . . . [a] person is subversive not only if he himself commits the specified acts but if he abets or advises another in aiding a third person to commit an act which will assist yet a fourth person in the overthrow or alteration of constitutional government. The Washington Supreme Court has said that knowledge is to be read into

---

[16] 377 U.S. 360 (1964).

71

every provision and we accept this construction. . . . But what is it that the Washington professor must "know"? Must he know that his aid or teaching will be used by another and that the person aided has the requisite guilty intent or is it sufficient that he know that his aid or teaching would or might be useful to others in the commission of acts intended to overthrow the government? Is it subversive activity, for example, to attend and participate in international conventions of mathematicians and exchange views with scholars from communist countries? What about the editor of a scholarly journal who analyzes and criticizes the manuscripts of communist scholars submitted for publication? Is selecting outstanding scholars from communist countries as visiting professors and advising, teaching, or consulting with them at the University of Washington a subversive activity if such scholars are known to be communists, or regardless of their affiliations, regularly teach students who are members of the Communist Party, which by statutory definition is subversive and dedicated to the overthrow of the government?

The Washington oath goes beyond overthrow or alteration by force or violence. It extends to alteration by "revolution" which, unless wholly redundant and its ordinary meaning distorted, includes any rapid or fundamental change. Would, therefore, any organization or any person . . . teaching peaceful but far-reaching constitutional amendments be engaged in subversive activity? Could one support the repeal of the Twenty-Second Amendment or participation by this country in a world government?

We also conclude that the . . . oath offends due process because of vagueness. The oath exacts a promise that the affiant will . . . promote respect for the flag and the institutions of the United States and the State of Washington. The range of activities which . . . might be deemed inconsistent with the required promise is very wide indeed. The teacher who refused to salute the flag or advocated refusal because of religious beliefs might well be accused of breaching his

72

promise. Cf. West Virginia State Board of Education v. Barnette, 319 U.S. 624. Even criticism of the design or color scheme of the state flag or unfavorable comparison of it with that of a sister State or foreign country could be deemed disrespectful and therefore violative of the oath. And what are "institutions" for the purposes of this oath? Is it every "practice, law, custom, and so on, which is a material and persistent element in the life or culture of an organized social group," or every "established society or corporation," every "establishment, esp[ecially] one of a public character"? The oath may prevent a professor from criticizing his state judicial system or the Supreme Court or the institution of judicial review. Or it might be deemed to proscribe advocating the abolition, for example, of the Civil Rights Commission, the House Committee on Un-American Activities, or foreign aid.

It is likewise difficult to ascertain what might be done without transgressing the promise to "promote . . . undivided allegiance to the government of the United States." It would not be unreasonable for the serious-minded oathtaker to conclude that he should dispense with lectures voicing far-reaching criticism of any . . . policy followed by the government of the United States. He could find it questionable under this language to ally himself with any interest group dedicated to opposing any current public policy or law of the federal government, for if he did, he might well be accused of placing loyalty to the group above allegiance to the United States.

Indulging every presumption of a narrow construction of the provisions of the . . . oath, consistent, however, with a proper respect for the English language, we cannot say that this oath provides an ascertainable standard of conduct or that it does not require more than a state may command under the guarantees of the First and Fourteenth Amendments.

One final harassment of faculty freedom is found in Slochower v. Board of Higher Education.[17] In this case the Charter of

[17] 350 U.S. 551 (1956).

the City of New York had a provision stating that any city employee who refused to answer the questions of a judge or legislative committee on the ground that his answers would tend to incriminate him would be terminated. Plaintiff was called before a United States Senate investigating committee. He told the committee that he was not a member of the communist party and offered to answer any questions concerning his activities after 1941, but refused to answer any dealing with the years 1940 and 1941 on Fifth Amendment grounds that his answers might be self-incrimnating. Shortly after testifying, he received notice of his suspension from Brooklyn College under the provisions of the city's charter. In support of the suspension the Board of Education claimed that only two inferences flowed from plaintiff's pleading the Fifth Amendment—either that answering the question put would tend to prove him guilty of a crime in some way connected with his official conduct, or that in order to avoid answering the question he falsely invoked the privilege by stating that the answer would tend to incriminate him. The plaintiff, on the other hand, claimed that this provision of the city charter imposed a penalty on him for exercising his constitutional rights.

Again we find that the court weighed society's interest in security and the individual's interest in freedom, and that the scales of justice tipped in favor of the individual. The court said:

> At the outset we must condemn the practice of imputing a sinister meaning to the exercise of a person's constitutional right under the Fifth Amendment. The right of an accused person to refuse to testify . . . was so important to our forefathers that they raised it to the dignity of a constitutional enactment, and it has been recognized as "one of the most valuable prerogatives of the citizen." . . . The privilege against self-incrimination would be reduced to a hollow mockery if its exercise could be taken as equivalent either to a confession of guilt or a conclusive presumption of perjury. . . . A witness may have a reasonable fear of prosecution and yet be innocent of any wrongdoing. The privilege serves to protect

74

the innocent who otherwise might be ensnared by ambiguous circumstances. . . .

As interpreted and applied by the state courts, [the provision] operates to discharge every city employee who invokes the Fifth Amendment. In practical effect the questions asked are taken as confessed and made the basis of the discharge. No consideration is given to such factors as the subject matter of the questions, remoteness of the period to which they are directed, or justification for exercise of the privilege. It matters not whether the plea resulted from mistake, inadvertence, or legal advice conscientiously given, whether wisely or unwisely. The heavy hand of the statute falls alike on all who exercise their constitutional privilege, the full enjoyment of which every person is entitled to receive.

Three justices dissented in the decision. They held that the city was reasonable in requiring its employees either to give evidence regarding facts of official conduct within their knowledge or to surrender their positions. In instances such as the Slochower case it is clear that reasonable men may disagree on what is reasonable. The judicial choice is not so much between right and wrong as between two rights, and there is no telling beyond contradiction which is more right. One wonders to what extent the state of law and order, war and peace, might make a difference. Perhaps it is easier to balance interests in favor of the individual in times of relative quiet. But there stands Barnette,[18] striking down the compulsory hand salute to the flag and pledge of allegiance statute, which was decided during the Second World War at a moment when it was not yet clear whether the United States war effort was "too little and too late."

[18] 319 U.S. 626 (1942).

75

THREE

Administration

Autonomy of the University

The university has long been referred to as a guild or republic of scholars. This description is a heritage from its origins. The university derives its name from the Latin *universitas* which in Roman law carried the connotation of a corporation. When professors and students were first drawn together in medieval times they formed a voluntary corporation. To do so they did not need the permission of civil authorities. They thus became a self-governing body and have continued to be so, more or less, throughout their history. As time passed they derived their charters from church or state, which did reserve some control over them. In the area of expertise such as law, medicine, theology, and the arts it seems only proper that experts should be self-governing, for who is to judge the exercise of expertise save the experts themselves? Yet, as expertise has a social incidence, society has an unquestionable stake in establishing and maintaining the university. Where to draw the line between autonomy and control, therefore, is a delicate matter.

Perhaps the most notable case dealing with this demarcation is Sterling v. Regents of University of Michigan.[1] The defendant had been directed by the legislature to discontinue its homeopathic medical college as a branch of the University in

[1] 110 Mich. 369—68 N.E. 253 (1896).

Ann Arbor and to transfer the college to the city of Detroit. The regents refused to do so and plaintiff sought to compel them. Defendants' defense was that such a transfer was not in the best interests of the university and, moreover, that it was not constitutional for the legislature to dictate the management of the university. The Supreme Court of the state sided with the regents, citing especially the provision of the state constitution that the regents should have the direction and control of all expenditures from the university interest fund. It interpreted this provision in favor of the university in the light of the history which led up to it. Under the constitution of 1835, it noted, the legislature had the entire control and management of the university, but the school did not prosper. Fluctuating majorities there led to frequent changes in university policy. New majorities were forever pulling the university up by the roots to see how it was growing whereas what it needed was the undisturbed growth so characteristic of private institutions where ultimate power was concentrated in the board of trustees. The framers of the constitution of 1850 were aware of these circumstances and sought to correct them by placing control of the university in a board of regents directly elected by the people. Since this was their purpose, it follows, as the court pointed out, that:

> *The board of regents and the legislature derive their power from the same supreme authority, namely, the [state] constitution. In so far as the powers of each are defined by that instrument, limitations are imposed, and a direct power conferred upon one necessarily excludes its existence in the other, in the absence of language showing the contrary intent. Neither the university nor the board of regents is mentioned in [the] article . . . which defines the powers and duties of the legislature. Nor in the article relating to the university and the board of regents is there any language which can be construed into conferring upon or reserving any control over that institution in the legislature. They are separate and distinct constitutional bodies, with the powers of the regents defined. By no rule of construction can it be held that either can encroach upon or exercise the powers conferred upon the other. . . .*

The Courts and Higher Education

In every case except that of the regents the constitution carefully and expressly reposes in the legislature the power to legislate and to control and define the duties of [the] corporations and officers. . . . No other conclusion . . . is possible than that the intention was to place this institution in the direct and exclusive control of the people themselves, through a constitutional body elected by them. As already shown, the maintenance of this power in the legislature would give to it the sole control and general supervision of the institution, and make the regents merely ministerial officers, with no other power than to carry into effect the general supervision which the legislature may see fit to exercise, or, in other words, to register its will. We do not think the constitution can bear that construction.

Public and Private Higher Education

Of all the occasions when colleges and universities have been before the courts there is probably no instance more notable than the famous Dartmouth College case. It behooves us to study this case, since it gave "solidarity and inviolability to the literary . . . . institutions of our country," as Chancellor James Kent, a great commentator on American law, once said. The issue raised by Dartmouth College v. Woodward,[2] whether public control can be exercised over a private college without its consent, had been building up for some time. It began with Harvard and Yale's sparring with the British crown over their initial charters. Originally both colleges had avoided royal charters for fear rights would be reserved to the crown which might have led to interference with the religious purposes for which they were founded. After the charter difficulties, several colleges had trouble with the endeavors of colonial legislatures to assert public control over them. The inclusion of governors as members of college boards of control eased this tension in several cases, but Dartmouth met the encroachment of New Hampshire head-on.

In the elections of 1816 in New Hampshire the Federalist

[2] 17 U.S. 518—4 Wheaton 518 (1819).

Party lost to the Jeffersonian Republicans. In order to make Dartmouth more submissive to the public will the new legislature passed a law amending the Dartmouth charter so as to transform the college into a university. The trustees of the college resisted and for a while there were two sets of officers on the campus, one for the college and the other for the university. As the latter had possession of the official seal, the former sued to recover it. The New Hampshire court, being of the same political complexion as the legislature, upheld the new statute. Daniel Webster, who had undertaken the brief for his alma mater, was not dismayed by the defeat. He carried the case to the United States Supreme Court where he argued that the act of the New Hampshire legislature was an impairment of the obligation of contract, forbidden by the Federal Constitution.

Chief Justice John Marshall, himself a Federalist like Webster, decided the case in favor of Dartmouth College but for reasons that are not widely known. Marshall had no difficulty in deciding that the Dartmouth charter was a contract, and therefore was entitled to the protection of the Federal Constitution unless it could be shown that Dartmouth College was a public rather than private institution of learning. In that case the State of New Hampshire would be fully justified in molding the college to its own purposes. From every angle he approached the issue, however, Marshall found Dartmouth a private rather than a public institution. The financial gifts for its support were private. Eleazar Wheelock, the founder, was not a public official. Furthermore, the beneficial interest in the founding of the college was directed toward the Indians; its benefits to the province were for youth in general, not New Hampshire youth in particular. Conclusive on this point was the location of Dartmouth, far from the centers of population of the time. Again, the fact that Dartmouth was incorporated by the crown did not make it a public corporation. Besides, the right to change the college was founded not on its being incorporated, but on its being an instrument of government and created for its purposes. Hence, any way he looked at the matter, Marshall concluded that Dartmouth was a charity-supported institution.

Before the American Revolution, the British parliament, he

recognized, might have repealed the Dartmouth charter and thereby forced the college to comply. But in this new country our Federal Constitution was designed to prevent the states from taking that sort of action. On the whole Marshall approved of this policy because:

> *It requires no very critical examination of the human mind to enable us to determine that one great inducement to these gifts is the conviction felt by the giver that the disposition he makes of them is immutable. It is probable that no man ever was, and that no man ever will be, the founder of a college, believing at the time that an act of incorporation constitutes no security for the institution; believing that it is immediately to be deemed a public institution whose funds are to be governed and applied not by the will of the donor, but by the will of the legislature. All such gifts are made in the pleasing, perhaps delusive hope that the charity will flow for ever in the channel which the givers have marked out for it. If every man finds in his own bosom strong evidence of the universality of this sentiment, there can be . . . little reason to imagine that the framers of our Constitution were strangers to it, and that, feeling the necessity and policy of giving permanence and security to contracts, of withdrawing them from the influence of legislative bodies whose fluctuating policy and repeated interferences produced the most perplexing and injurious embarrassments, they still deemed it necessary to leave these contracts subject to those interferences. The motives for such an exception must be very powerful to justify the construction which makes it.*

Defendant apparently argued that in the future it might be necessary to alter the original purposes of the college and that since New Hampshire had now stepped into the shoes of the original grantor, George III, that state was better fitted than private trustees to perform the alteration. Marshall saw little merit in this contention.

> *We should believe that learned and intelligent men,*

80

selected . . . for the government of a literary institution, would select learned and intelligent men for their successors; men as well fitted for the government of a college as those who might be chosen by other means. Should this reasoning ever prove erroneous, in a particular case, public opinion . . . would correct the institution. The mere possibility of the contrary would not justify a construction of the Constitution which should exclude these contracts from the protection of the provision whose terms comprehend them.

Not everyone was happy with his reasoning. Before the Chief Justice had handed down his decision, Thomas Jefferson took an opposite view. "The idea that institutions established for the use of the nation," he wrote the governor of New Hampshire, "cannot be touched or modified even to make them answer their end, because of rights gratuitously supposed in those employed to manage them in trust for the public, may, perhaps, be a salutary provision against the abuses of a monarch but it is most absurd against the nation itself."[3] The prosperity of the college, others asserted, depended on the public esteem in which the college was held. If this esteem was impaired by public mistrust it would avail the college nothing to successfully maintain in court that the public will was misdirected.

One of the reasons for the dissatisfaction with private colleges had been their rather exclusive and unyielding emphasis on a classical curriculum. Major relief from the frustration of the Dartmouth College Case, which prevented redirection of curricula, came when the federal government passed the first Morrill Act. This act granted public lands for the establishment of colleges emphasizing agricultural and mechanical arts. Most states established institutions of their own with these funds, but Connecticut gave them to Yale which went to considerable expense in enlarging its Sheffield Scientific School for the new curriculum. Thirty years later the federal government passed a second Morrill Act with new appropriations. In view of the earlier commitment Yale expected to receive these funds too, but coincident with this new federal act Connecticut de-

[3] Cited in Charles Warren, *The Supreme Court in United States History* (Boston: Little, Brown, 1922), Vol. 1, p. 484.

cided to found a state university of its own and to divert the new funds to the nourishment of this institution. Yale sued the state treasurer to prevent this diversion and to have the funds paid into its treasury. In the resulting case of Yale College v. Sanger[4] the decision hinged on legal technicalities which need not concern us, but the court did spin off an incidental remark which is of considerable significance since it shows that a state can change its mind in spite of obligations to private institutions.

It is not absolutely necessary at this time to consider the alleged rights of the complainant to the annual appropriations which are being made by the United States under the act of 1890, and which will amount in time to $25,000 annually; but I am not willing, by silence, to have it inferred that I absolutely concur in the position of the complainant's college [that] by its endowment, under the federal statute of 1862, the State of Connecticut has no power to establish another college under the provisions of that act, or to make any other disposition of the appropriations under the federal statute of 1890 than those which it had specified in the state statute of 1863. The complainant's counsel think that having selected an appointee the state had, under the United States act of 1890, no new power to select another appointee or to endow it; and that the power of appropriation was exhausted; and that, as to colleges which had been established under the act of 1862, the appropriations under the act of 1890 are directly for their benefit and not for the benefit of new institutions. The provisions of the act are vaguely expressed, and a construction of the statute is postponed until a decision is necessary.

Religion

Because pluralism has long characterized religious culture in America, this country has had a tradition of separation of church and state. This tradition is incorporated into the First Amendment

---

[4] 62 Fed. 177 (1894).

of the Federal Constitution forbidding an establishment of religion, and in the state constitutions forbidding the expenditure of tax monies for any form of sectarian instruction. These constitutional provisions do not mean that America is anti-religious but rather that metaphysical and theological beliefs are so profoundly and irreconcilably diverse that to escape religious orthodoxy on the one hand and political tyranny on the other, it is necessary to yield to secularism in tax-supported education.

To avoid a resulting religious illiteracy some state universities have offered courses in the Bible as literature. To guard against its being taught as religion, this course at the University of Washington was assigned to the English department. In Calvary Bible Presbyterian Church v. Regents of University of Washington,[5] plaintiff was not satisfied and complained that teaching the Bible as literature had inescapable religious overtones. The trial court found that the course

> *concerns itself with the literary features of the Bible and, as a necessary part thereof, the history of ancient Israel; the authorship and treatment of the various books of the Bible, and their interpretation from a literary and an historical point of view, employing the same techniques of scholarship used in the study of any other literary or historical text; that the course is offered as part of a secular program of education to advance the knowledge of students and the learning of mankind; that it is taught by members of the English department who are competent literary scholars, qualified to teach in their respective fields of specialization. The course is not taught by theologians. One professor uses the Revised Standard Version of the Bible; another the Oxford Annotated Edition of the Revised Standard Version; a third the King James version. Each makes his choice of the English translation for his own professional reasons.*

After reviewing these facts the appellate court concluded:

> *The sole question remaining is whether the conclusions*

[5] 71 Wash. 2nd 912—436 P. 2nd 189 (1967).

of law based upon the findings are violative of the constitutional provisions. . . .

The touchstone of the problem is the meaning attributed to "religious . . . instruction" as used in . . . our constitution. It must be kept in mind that the words appear after two more specific terms: "worship" and "exercise." This, we believe, is an indication that the framers of our constitution did not intend the word "instruction" to be construed without limit, but that the proscribed field be confined to that category of instruction . . . [that is] devotional in nature and designed to induce faith and belief in the student.

There can be no doubt that our constitutional bars are absolute against religious instruction and indoctrination in specific religious beliefs or dogma; but they do not proscribe open, free, critical, and scholarly examination of the literature, experiences, and knowledge of mankind. If they did, many fields of scholarship—anthropology, zoology, the theory of evolution, astronomy, the germ theory of disease and medical cure, to mention only a few—would have to be removed from our university. It might be said that the objective examination of these theories conflicts with the religious beliefs of certain persons entertaining contrary beliefs based on their religious convictions. This would, indeed, be true "sectarian control or influence," which is prohibited by . . . our constitution.

The result advocated by plaintiffs would be catastrophic in the field of higher education. Would plaintiffs have us strike the works of Milton, Dante, and the other ancient authors whose writings have survived the ages, because they wrote of religious theories with which plaintiffs quarrel? Our constitution does not guarantee sectarian control of our educational system.

Telescoping their testimony, we find that [the course] was taught in a completely objective manner; had no effect on religious beliefs; was not slanted toward any particular theological or religious point of view; did not indoctrinate anyone; did not enter into the realm of belief or faith; and was not taught from a religious point of view.

One judge, however, remained apart from the majority. Noting that there are two views of the Bible—the traditional view that the Bible is the revealed word of God and the liberal view that man is free to judge the genuineness and authority of the Bible—he thought teaching "the Bible as literature" had a built in way of favoring the latter view. Citing earlier precedents of the Washington court he held religious instruction objectionable even though it was not sectarian, denominational, or doctrinal, and even though it covered only history, biography, narrative, and literary features.

The question of public support of sectarian higher education came out on a much larger scale in Horace Mann League v. Board of Public Works.[6] In this case the State of Maryland had appropriated $2.5 million for the erection of buildings on the campuses of four church-related colleges within the state. Plaintiff contended that the appropriation was a violation of provisions already mentioned in federal and state constitutions. The league conceded that a college might have some degree of relation to religion or to a church without being designated sectarian but in this instance it claimed the connection was too substantial. Defendant contended that even if the relation was substantial, the appropriation was not unconstitutional. To determine whether the connection was or was not substantial the court laid down the following criteria:

> *The experts on both sides are in general accord that the following factors are significant in determining whether an educational institution is religious or sectarian: (1) the stated purposes of the college; (2) the college personnel, which includes the governing board, the administrative officers, the faculty, and the student body (with considerable stress being laid on the substantiality of religious control over the governing board . . .); (3) the college's relationship with religious organizations, . . . which . . . includes the extent of owner-*

[6] 242 Md. 645—220 A. 2nd 15 (1965).

ship, financial assistance, the college's memberships and affilia-
tions, religious purposes, and miscellaneous aspects of the col-
lege's relationship with its sponsoring church; (4) the place
of religion in the college's program, which includes the extent
of religious manifestation in the physical surroundings, the
character and extent of religious observance sponsored or en-
couraged by the college, the required participation for any or
all students, the extent to which the college sponsors or encour-
ages religious activity of sects different from that of the col-
lege's own church, and the place of religion in the curriculum
and in extra-curricular programs; (5) the result . . . of the
college program, such as accreditation and the nature and
character of the activities of the alumni; and (6) the work
and image of the college in the community.

Applying these principles the court approved the appropriation for one of the four colleges but denied it to the other three.
Three judges, however, were more liberal and would have sustained
the appropriation for all four. According to their reasoning,

The factors of (a) a rapidly expanding population of
the state and the country, (b) an increasing proportion of that
part of the population of college age which attends college, and
(c) an ever more complex society which requires ever more
highly developed skills of more people in order to supply indi-
viduals competent to conduct the affairs of government and
the private economy and furnish professional and scientific
services have strained college facilities, physical and human,
to the limit, if not beyond, and will combine to require more
and more such facilities. Private colleges furnish a most signifi-
cant help in offering the collegiate and graduate training now
available. It is said that there are some two thousand private
institutions of higher learning in the country, of which eight
hundred are church-related. . . . If they are to continue to
do their part and bear the new load of increased enrollments,
they must have new facilities and, since private colleges tradi-

tionally have financial problems which limit their expansion, most of the cost of new facilities must come from government.

A recent decision of a three judge federal district court in Tilton v. Finch,[7] in which the facts were almost identical, rejected the reasoning of the Maryland court. Rather than determine whether the college recipient as a whole was secular, the federal court inquired only whether the primary purpose and effect of the specific subsidy was secular. Not unlike the minority in the Maryland case the federal court unanimously held:

> *Applying the secular purpose and primary effect test to the act . . . in question, we find that it clearly meets the first requirement of a secular legislative purpose. It contains a congressional declaration that the policy underlying the act is to increase the student enrollment capacity of the nation's institutions of higher education through grants for construction of academic facilities . . .*
>
> *The Act also meets the second requirement of a primary effect that neither advances nor inhibits religion. The focus of this test . . . is the function, secular or religious, which the government aid subsidizes—not the nature of the institution, secular or religious, which receives the aid.*

One critic, in his disappointment with the Maryland case, said that he did not think a court of law was a suitable agency for determining the secular or sectarian flavor of a college. In place of the foregoing criteria this critic suggested three new ones. He would give no public funds to a sectarian college if the college was not approved by a regional accrediting association, if it penalized scholarly inquiry, or if it conferred automatic sectarian priority on students for either admission or graduation.[8] An indication of the way this automatic discrimination might work is found in Carr v. St.

[7] 312 Fed. Supp. 1191 (1970).
[8] L. Averill, "Sectarian Higher Education and the Public Interest," *Journal of Higher Education,* 1969, *40,* 85–100.

John's University, New York.[9] Plaintiffs were Catholic students at the Roman Catholic defendant university. Before graduating they got married in a civil ceremony with two other Catholic students as witnesses. According to canon law they should have been married by a priest, and for this breach of discipline all four students were dismissed from the university. They took exception to this treatment, especially since one of them had completed all his work for a degree and was about to graduate. A five judge court divided three to two in favor of the defendant. The majority held,

> *The regulation on discipline provides that, "In conformity with the ideals of Christian education and conduct, the university reserves the right to dismiss a student at any time on whatever grounds the university judges advisable." To the Catholic students and authorities at the university, "Christian education and conduct" meant and means "Catholic education and conduct." The petitioners do not claim that they understood it to mean anything else, nor do they claim that they did not understand what they were doing or the consequences of their act in the eyes of their Church. . . .*
>
> *When a university, in expelling a student, acts within its jurisdiction, not arbitrarily but in the exercise of an honest discretion based on facts within its knowledge that justify the exercise of discretion, a court may not review the exercise of its discretion. . . . Here, the discretion exercised by the university was of that character.*

The minority held otherwise:

> *In our opinion . . . there was no basis for the university's exercise of discretion to dismiss these petitioners. The university is a public institution, chartered by the state, open to persons of all religious faiths, and engaged in providing secular learning leading to a general academic degree. Such a university may not enforce against a student an ecclesiastical law, the breach of which is not immoral according to the*

[9] 231 N.Y.S. 2nd 410 (1962).

standards of society in general, or which it does not enforce equally against all students at the university, whether Catholic or non-Catholic.

Conflict with Private Business

The conduct of colleges and universities is generally recognized as beneficial to the social environment in which they operate. Sometimes, however, what is recognized as beneficial to the academic community is seen as harmful to the business one. Two instances will be sufficient to make the point and to indicate how the conflict is resolved. Gott v. Berea[10] is doubly worth examining because it also is notable for its statement of the doctrine that the college stands *in loco parentis* to its students. In this case plaintiff conducted a restaurant across the street from defendant college, which had issued a manual in which its students were admonished not to enter saloons, gambling houses, eating houses, or places of amusement not controlled by the college, on pain of immediate dismissal. In spite of this rule several of the students patronized the restaurant and were consequently expelled. The plaintiff alleged that the reasons given in chapel for the inclusion of eating houses in the rule was that he was a bootlegger and had been convicted of the illegal sale of liquor. He charged the school with slandering him and maliciously conspiring to injure his business. The college justified its rule on the ground that its students were of slender means and unaccustomed to the temptations of even a small town; hence, to keep the students at their studies and to save their money, the rule was necessary. In no event was it directed against the plaintiff.

The court immediately stated,

The larger question . . . is whether the rule . . . was a reasonable one, and within the power of the college authorities to enact, and the further question whether, in that event, appellant Gott will be heard to complain. That the enforcement of the rule worked a great injury to Gott's restau-

[10] 156 Ky. 376—161 S.E. 204 (1913).

rant business cannot well be denied, but unless he can show that the college authorities have been guilty of a breach of some legal duty which they owe to him, he has no cause of action against them for the injury. . . . It is a well-established principle that when a lawful act is performed in the proper manner, the party performing it is not liable for mere incidental consequences injuriously resulting from it to another. . . .

College authorities stand in loco parentis *concerning the physical and moral welfare and mental training of the pupils, and we are unable to see why to that end they may not make any rule or regulation for the government or betterment of their pupils that a parent could for the same purpose. Whether the rules or regulations are wise, or their aims worthy, is a matter left solely to the discretion of the authorities, or parents as the case may be, and in the exercise of that discretion the courts are not disposed to interfere, unless the rules and aims are unlawful or against public policy. . . .*

Of course this rule is not intended to, nor will it be permitted to interfere with parental control of children in the home, unless the acts forbidden materially affect the conduct and discipline of the school.

There is nothing in the case to show that the college had any contract, business, or other direct relations with the appellant. They owed him no special duty, and while he may have suffered an injury yet he does not show that the college is a wrong-doer. . . . Nor does he show that in enacting the rules they did it unlawfully, or that they exceeded their power, or that there was any conspiracy to do anything unlawful.

Gott v. Berea involved a private college. Nevertheless a similar result was reached in Villyard v. Regents of the University of Georgia,[11] in which a public university was the defendant. The facts here were that the university provided a laundry and dry cleaning service at reduced prices not only for students but for fac-

[11] 204 Ga. 517—50 S.E. 2nd 313 (1948).

ulty and other employees as well. Plaintiffs claimed that this action not only harmed their business but was unfair since the institution was using rent-free property in competition with private enterprise. After enunciating the principle that "the right to protect a public educational institution and its student body is equal to or superior to the right of . . . a merchant desiring to deal with such institution or its students," the court noted its application to a variety of activities:

> *In other jurisdictions, enterprises held to be reasonably related to the education, welfare, and health of student bodies, and therefore not to constitute unfair competition, include the following: cafeterias, . . . rental of school property, . . . [book stores], . . . a university press, . . . a recreation center, . . . a university infirmary, . . . manufacture and distribution of hog-cholera serum to farmers and swine-growers at cost. . . .*
>
> *Applying the above legal principles to the facts of the present case, if the operation of the laundry and dry cleaning service . . . is lawful, it matters not that such enterprise is competitive with the plaintiffs' business. "When free public schools were first established, they competed with and ultimately drove from the field numerous private schools, but those who conducted the private schools could not complain of unfair competition since the state had the right to establish the free school system. Universities and colleges established by the states are in direct competition with privately controlled colleges, but the competition is not unfair nor unlawful because the state has the power to establish its universities and colleges, and to support them by taxation."*

Academic Personnel as Public Officials

Often one casually refers to the faculty or administration of state colleges and universities as officials of these institutions, but more care should be used in making this appellation. The reason for greater caution comes out very clearly in two cases. In the first,

Hartigan v. Regents of West Virginia University,[12] plaintiff alleged that he was capriciously and maliciously removed from his professorship without being given any notice. Whether he was entitled to notice turned on whether he was a public official or just an employee of the university. Before coming to that issue, however, the judge doubted that it should even take jurisdiction in this case. Said he:

> *The proposition is asserted that every action of the regents may be made the subject of judicial review. That is what it amounts to practically. When a professor is to be removed, he must have notice, trial, and some writ from a circuit court upon the theory of erroneous action by the regents to review that trial, and then an appeal to the Supreme Court. When the case is before the board of regents, under this theory, he must be allowed to have witnesses and counsel for full defense. So the case may be made one of almost interminable litigation, to the great harm of the university; and every case of removal may—probably would—be made the subject of protracted litigation. In the meanwhile the incompetent professor would go on, and the harm to the university would be, or might be, very great. Under this theory the courts would control the board of regents, would paralyse the arm of the executive, deprive the executive of its power over the university, plainly conferred by the legislature. Thus the courts would practically exercise jurisdiction over the university, administer its affairs in greater or less degree, according as the litigations might be few or numerous, notwithstanding the code plainly intended to put its government in the hands of the regents. . . . I am ready to disclaim the assumption of this power, which I would consider little less than usurpation. It would be an invasion of the functions of the executive department. There is no jurisdiction in this or any court to control the administerial action of the executive.*

[12] 49 W.Va. 14—38 S.E. 698 (1901).

Administration

This objection notwithstanding, the judge did go on to dispose of plaintiff's right to notice before dismissal:

I hold that [plaintiff] . . . had no right to notice because he is not a public officer but a mere employee of the board of regents. . . . The university is a corporation and considering it merely in that light, it is clear that the board can remove its employees at pleasure, for the officers or employees of a corporation have no franchise or property in their offices, but are simply ministerial agents to carry out its corporate business. . . . What is a public office? The word is used in so many senses that it is impossible to give a precise definition covering all cases. It depends not on what we call it, or even on what a statute may incidentally call it, but upon the powers wielded, the functions performed, and other circumstances manifesting the character of the position. . . . "The most important characteristic which distinguishes an office from an employment or contract is that the creation or conferring of an office involves a delegation to the individual of some of the sovereign functions of government, to be exercised by him for the benefit of the public; that some portion of the sovereignty of the country, either legislative, executive, or judicial, attaches, for the time being, to be exercised for the public benefit."
. . . I ask, what part of the sovereignty of the state does a professor in a college exercise? "Office is a public station or employment conferred by the government, and embraces the idea of tenure, duration. emolument, and duties." . . . A professor of the university has not what is called tenure in office, no fixed term. What he is paid makes him no officer. A mere employee is paid. That an official oath is required by law is a sign of office, and our code prescribes it as to officers, but does not require a professor to take it. Where a statute prescribes specific duties for an office, it is a strong circumstance that an office is intended; but the code prescribes none for a professor. Chief Justice Marshall . . . said: "Although an office is an employment, it does not follow that every employ-

93

ment is an office." . . . *I say a professor, learned and distinguished as he may be, is an employee and subordinate of the board of regents, in law.*

Extending this principle further, the supreme court of Wisconsin held that not even the president of its state university was an officer. In Martin v. Smith[13] the president of the University of Wisconsin was appointed to administer the federal Selective Service Act during the Second World War and the board of regents approved a leave of absence for him. However, as Wisconsin had a statute declaring that no one in the state could hold both state and federal offices at the same time, the defendant treasurer refused to pay the warrants for the president's salary. The court, on the contrary, directed the defendant to pay the warrants on the ground that the president, although undoubtedly a federal official, was not a state official. Indeed, not even his being a member of the board of regents, who were state officers, made him a public official. Expecting surprise at this result, the court added,

It may seem anomalous to some that the president of a great university should not be a public officer while a justice of the peace or a notary public is a public officer. However, the character of the employment is not determined by the salary paid to the employee or by the importance of the duties which he performs or by the manner in which he is chosen, but rather by the nature of the duties he performs. In the case of the president of the university, the nature of these duties much more nearly conforms to the nature of the duties of a superintendent of schools than it does to the nature of the duties performed by a public officer. He is an employee, not a public officer; he holds a position, not an office of trust, profit, or honor under the state.

Insubordination

Success in college and university administration puts a premium on effective team work. The leader must realize that effective

[13] 239 Wis. 314—N.W. 2nd 163 (1941).

team work allows some room for loyal opposition among members of the team. Nevertheless, occasions arise when the opposition is disloyal and uncooperative. Yet just when is opposition loyal and when is it disloyal or insubordinate? Insubordination is probably a question of fact more than one of law but in either event difficult to prove, as seen in State v. Regents of University of Nevada.[14] After notice and hearing before the board of regents, the petitioner, chairman of the department of biology and president of the local chapter of the American Association of University Professors, was severed from his employment. Naturally aggrieved he sought a court review of his removal. The main thrust of the controversy seemed to center on the fact that petitioner had circulated among the university faculty an article by Arthur Bestor entitled "Aimlessness in Education," which was a sharp diatribe against the professional study of education. Petitioner stated that his purpose in distributing the article was to attack the question of low admission standards of the university, an issue vigorously debated in campus circles at the time. The president of the university, however, also regarded distribution of the article as an indirect attack on himself personally, since he had taken his Ph.D. in education.

It may be appropriate to point out parenthetically that this incident at the University of Nevada occurred at a time shortly after the Second World War when critics were making a concerted attack on the inadequacies of the American school system and blaming them on the professional study of education. Bestor's invective, irony, sarcasm, and name-calling provoked many more educators than just the president of the University of Nevada. Even petitioner recognized the one-sided quality of the article and called his colleagues' attention to it through published critiques. At the hearing before the board of regents members of the faculty who read it indicated various reactions but none, not even the head of the department of education, considered it very seriously.

The court found that petitioner's conduct had violated no rule of the defendant. If anything, his actions lay inside, not outside, official policy as enunciated by the president's predecessor in office,

[14] 70 Nev. 347—269 P. 2nd 265 (1954).

95

who had said that all ideas should be considered on their merits, without reference to their source, and that minority groups should be encouraged in their study to test and refine group thought and expression.

The court came to a conclusion opposite to the regents and therefore instituted its judgment in place of theirs, saying,

> *With full recognition of the right of the regents to weigh the evidence, to resolve conflicts in such evidence, to pass upon the credibility of the witnesses, to commit procedural errors not going to the jurisdiction, and to be the finders of facts relevant to the issues, the observations made in this opinion inevitably point to the conclusion that the record presents no substantial support of either the finding of insubordination or the finding of the lack of cooperation and presents no cause for removal.*

Gifts

It is a commonplace that private citizens make charitable donations to colleges and universities. The financial needs of higher education, however, have constantly tended to outstrip support and, important as small donations are when lumped together, there has been a growing need for more substantial gifts. The recent gradual transition of the control of wealth from individual to corporate hands has pointed to industrial and commercial corporations as one possible source for new funding. The Smith Manufacturing Company made financial contributions to the support of Princeton University, and some of the company's stockholders challenged this action as beyond the corporate powers set forth in its charter. The company, they alleged, was incorporated to pay dividends to stockholders, not to make charitable contributions to eleemosynary institutions. To test whether the company had broad or narrow powers, Smith Manufacturing Company v. Barlow[15] was prepared for the courts.

In defense of the company's action its president pointed out

[15] 13 N.J. 145—98 A. 2nd 581 (1953).

96

that contributions like the one to Princeton created a favorable community environment for its business, to say nothing of assuring it a flow of well trained personnel with a liberal education. Moreover, he cited other industrialists to the effect that the continued existence of private colleges was a necessary complement to the private enterprise system. Delving into legal lore the court found the company's gift not only sanctioned by New Jersey statutory law but by the common law as well. In the latter connection the court alluded to precedent for the Smith Company's gift as far back as the beginning of the eighteenth century to a publication in which

the author stated flatly that "The general intent and end of all civil incorporations is for better government." And he pointed out that the early corporate charters . . . furnish additional support for the notion that the corporate object was the public one of managing and ordering the trade as well as the private one of profit for the members. . . . However, with later economic and social developments and the free availability of the corporate device for all trades, the end of private profit became generally accepted as the controlling one in all businesses other than those classed broadly as public utilities. . . . As a concomitant the common-law rule developed that those who managed the corporation could not disburse any corporate funds for philanthropic or other worthy public cause unless the expenditure would benefit the corporation. . . . During the nineteenth century when corporations were relatively few and small and did not dominate the country's wealth, the common-law rule did not significantly interfere with the public interest. But the twentieth century has presented a different climate. . . . Control of economic wealth has passed largely from individual entrepreneurs to dominating corporations, and calls upon the corporations for reasonable philanthropic donations have come to be made with increased public support. In many instances such contributions have been sustained by the courts within the common-law doctrine upon liberal findings that the donations tended reasonably to promote the corporate objectives. . . .

The Courts and Higher Education

It seems to us that just as the conditions prevailing when corporations were originally created required that they serve public as well as private interests, modern conditions require that corporations acknowledge and discharge social as well as private responsibilities as members of the communities within which they operate. Within this broad concept there is no difficulty in sustaining, as incidental to their proper objects and in aid of the public welfare, the power of corporations to contribute corporate funds within reasonable limits in support of academic institutions. But even if we confine ourselves to the terms of the common-law rule in its application to current conditions, such expenditures may likewise readily be justified as being for the benefit of the corporation; indeed, if need be the matter may be viewed strictly in terms of actual survival of the corporation in a free enterprise system.

Taxes

Cases involving higher education and taxation are legion. Only three are chosen here and these because they relate directly to the academic's pocketbook when making out his income tax return. All three cases deal with the issue of whether expenses incurred in study and research are deductible items. In the first case, Hill v. Commissioner of Internal Revenue,[16] the plaintiff was a high school teacher who attended summer school at Columbia University and sought an income tax deduction for her expenses. She was head of the department of English in her high school and held the highest teaching certificate issued by her State of Virginia. This certificate, however, was about to expire. To renew it and thus assure the continuity of her appointment she had the option of presenting college credits for work done in academic or professional subjects or of passing an examination on five books selected by the State Board of Education. The Commissioner of Internal Revenue disallowed a deduction for expenses at Columbia because the teacher had not shown that going to summer school was the usual method of renewing a certificate and because she had not shown that she was

---

[16] 181 Fed. 2nd 906 (1950).

98

under contract to continue as a teacher at the time she took the summer work. Moreover the commissioner implied that the teacher's expenses were of a personal rather than a business character for the astounding reason that she had frankly admitted she had enjoyed the summer school work.

The court was inclined to think that the commissioner's obvious distaste for this kind of deduction had led him to be unnecessarily critical and brushed his objections aside. It quoted,

> "*The dues paid by teachers to professional societies, the price of their subscriptions for educational journals connected with their profession, and the expenses . . . incurred in attending teachers' conventions . . . are considered ordinary and necessary business expenses and are deductible . . . for federal income tax purposes.*" . . . *Teachers generally could probably pursue [their] teaching careers without being [members] of a professional society, without subscribing to educational journals, and without attending conventions of teachers. Yet this taxpayer went to Columbia prompted by the necessity of renewing her certificate as a prerequisite to continuing her work as a teacher in the . . . school. . . . The initiation fee required to be paid . . . to a labor union in order to obtain employment represents an ordinary and necessary business expense and . . . may be deduced. . . . How much stronger in favor of deductibility and more persuasive are the facts in the case of the instant taxpayer!*

If anyone thought that in spite of the more flexible opinion of the court some ambiguity yet remained on the question of employment, that uncertainty was laid to rest in the subsequent case of Furner v. Commissioner of Internal Revenue.[17] The plaintiff, convinced that her future teaching required greater depth of training than she possessed, gave up her position (not even taking a leave of absence) in order to devote herself full-time to graduate study. After a year of no teaching duties she took new employment and

[17] 393 Fed. 2nd 292 (1968).

sought to deduct the expenses of her year of study. The Commissioner disallowed the deductions because, he said, plaintiff was not engaged in the business of teaching during that year and therefore could not claim her expenses as business deductions.

The court quickly concentrated on the legal significance of the fact that plaintiff was not on leave during her year of graduate study, stating its opinion that,

> *Apparently the commissioner and the tax court accord controlling importance to whether a teacher's period of study (expenses for which would otherwise qualify for deduction) interrupts the regularity of the teacher's employment as a teacher during successive school years, following the traditional pattern. Enrollment for study is not deemed to interrupt regularity (1) if undertaken during the traditional vacation periods, (2) if the study is part time during a school year while the teacher is also performing teaching duties, or (3) if the study is full time during a school year, but an employment relationship technically continues by virtue of leave, granted by the employing school.*
>
> *The governing statute is the very general provision allowing deduction of "ordinary and necessary expenses paid or incurred . . . in carrying on any trade or business. . . ." The commissioner and tax court put too much emphasis, we think, on whether the course of study displaces performance of teaching activity, . . . and give insufficient consideration to the broader question whether the relationship of the course of study to intended future performance as a teacher is such that the expenses thereof can reasonably be considered ordinary and necessary in carrying on the business of teaching. Factors which make it advantageous to undertake the course of study in a single year rather than to spread it out over several summers are surely relevant.*
>
> *The tax court's finding, based as it was on the fact petitioner was not on leave, is clearly erroneous.*

Much the same issue was involved in Brooks v. Commissioner

of Internal Revenue,[18] where the applicant for tax relief had been engaged in research instead of teaching. The plaintiff had incurred expenses while doing research in Europe, and when the expense account was disallowed the issue centered on whether she was engaged in business during this period so that her expenses could appear as incidental to her business. There was no question that she was well established in the field of research, for over the years she had received a number of subsidies from foundations as well as university appointments. The commissioner admitted plaintiff's outlay as ordinary and necessary expense but contended that there was not a sufficient profit motive to indicate that they had been incurred in a trade or business nor were they necessary to keep petitioner from losing the small stipend she had been receiving from the university. He viewed these expenditures in the nature of a "capital investment —that what she was in fact doing was equivalent to getting further education in order to increase her future profit potential rather than presently engaging in a profitable enterprise."

The court took a more liberal view than the commissioner and allowed the deduction, stating,

> *In view of (1) the stipulated facts in this case; (2) the admission by the government "that in order to adequately perform her research duties it was necessary for her to travel to Europe;" . . . (3) [the fact that] she was required by her contract to engage in continuous research; (4) the profit she had derived in previous years from her research and her undisputed testimony that she expected to derive profit in the future; (5) the fact that these expenses were incurred in her sole present activity, research, and not for the purpose of gaining any other or better job; (6) the many years spent by petitioner in similar research throughout the world . . . we conclude the tax court erred in concluding that the petitioner was not engaged in a "trade or business." We hold all her admittedly accurate travel expenses were "ordinary and necessary travel expenses" incurred in connection with her business of research.*

[18] 274 Fed. 2nd 96 (1959).

The Courts and Higher Education

The proper test is not the reasonableness of the taxpayer's belief that a profit will be realized, but whether it is entered into and carried on in good faith for the purpose of making a profit, or in the belief that a profit can be realized thereon, and that it is not conducted merely for pleasure, exhibition, or social diversion.

FOUR

Academic Program

Curriculum

Not many cases arise where courts are asked to decide questions involving the heart of higher education—its academic program and standards. Such questions are usually within the competence of the faculty and administration. Nevertheless, a few cases have come up which may whet curiosity. The first of these, Lesser v. Board of Education,[1] involved an able young high school student who was eager to prepare himself for college. His chances of success, his high school advisor informed him, would be greatly enhanced if he enrolled in a special scholarship program designed for the more able and industrious student. This he did and finally graduated with a scholastic average of 84.3. Brooklyn College, where he wanted to go, required a grade of at least 85 for admission and consequently refused to take him. The boy's mother thought her son's average should be reviewed in light of the fact that he took the special rather than the regular program. Hence she brought this action to compel the high school and college to get together and correct the boy's record.

The lower court granted the relief sought by the mother, taking the stand that it had a right to review the discretionary act of an administrative officer when exercised arbitrarily or capriciously. To the lower court

[1] 239 N.Y.S. 2nd 776 (1963).

103

it was unreasonable to prevent a boy going to the college of his choice by reason of a deficit of seven/tenths of one per cent. The appeal court, on the contrary, found no abuse of administrative discretion. Petitioner's son had received uniform treatment along with the rest of the applicants. Indeed, to have advanced his average would have been truly unfair since there were 170 other applicants with grades above his and still below 85.

> *In our opinion, the court was without power to make such directions. Courts may not interfere with the administrative discretion exercised by agencies which are vested with the administration and control of educational institutions, unless the circumstances disclosed by the record leave no scope for the use of that discretion in the manner under scrutiny. . . .*
>
> *More particularly, a court should refrain from interjecting its views within those delicate areas of school administration which relate to the eligibility of applicants and the determination of marking standards, unless clear abuse of statutory authority or a practice of discrimination or gross error has been shown. . . .*
>
> *The record before us denotes no arbitrary, unfair, or unreasonable conduct by the appellants in denying admission.*
>
> *Whether in computing the high school average the marks given in special courses such as the "Scholarship Program" should be accorded more weight than the marks given in standard courses was clearly a matter resting exclusively in the discretion of the school and college authorities. Equally, the determination as to what factors should enter into the standards set for college admission was within the exclusive province of the college authorities. The judicial task ends when it is found that the applicant has received from college authorities uniform treatment under reasonable regulations fairly administered.*

The next case, Columbia University v. Jacobsen,[2] reads almost like a college prank and yet it raises a semantic distinction that

[2] 148 A. 2nd 63 (1959).

must not be overlooked. The trustees accepted a promissory note from a student in payment of his college tuition. Subsequently the student refused payment because, he alleged, the university had promised in catalogues and brochures to teach him such virtues as wisdom, understanding, character, courage, justice, and liberty, and had obviously not done so since it refused to graduate him because of low scholastic standing. The trustees took the student to court, where he ultimately boiled down his complaint to the charge that Columbia did not teach wisdom as it claimed to. The trustees admitted allegiance to the virtues named but insisted that the university had made no misrepresentation about them to the student.

Defendant was right, of course, in sensing a pedagogical distinction between teaching knowledge and teaching wisdom. Knowledge can be taught in college but wisdom can only be learned in life. The court saved the day for Columbia by pointing out that no college in its right mind would ever confuse these two ideas:

Wisdom is not a subject which can be taught and . . . no rational person would accept such a claim made by any man or institution. We find nothing in the record to establish that Columbia represented, expressly or even by way of impression, that it could or would teach wisdom or the several qualities which defendant insists are "synonyms for or aspects of the same quality." The matter is perhaps best summed up in the supporting affidavit of the dean of Columbia College, where he said that "All that any college can do through its teachers, libraries, laboratories, and other facilities is to endeavor to teach the student the known facts, acquaint him with the nature of those matters which are unknown, and thereby assist him in developing mentally, morally, and physically. Wisdom is a hoped-for end product of education, experience, and ability which many seek and many fail to attain."

It is a question, moreover, whether defendant had ever put himself in a mood to learn what Columbia had to teach. Admonished by the dean for his low scholastic standing, defendant wrote him a lengthy letter in which he said, "I want to learn, but I must do it my own way. I realize my behavior is nonconforming, but in these times when there are so many forces that demand conformity, I hope I will find Columbia willing to grant some freedom to a student who wants to be a literary artist." What a foreshadowing this case was of the subsequent decade in American higher education.

The third case, Printup v. Wick,[3] was also based on breach of contract. The catalogue of St. Cloud State College called for an academic year of 172 days but did not define what an academic day was. Ordinarily the academic day was taken up with conventional subject matter courses like history, economics, psychology, political science, and the like. For one day, however, defendant permitted a program called "Time Out Today," which replaced the usual subject matter curriculum with a curriculum organized around such lively issues as the draft, war, sex, the politics of protest, and so on. Special speakers and films were brought on the campus for the occasion. Plaintiffs particularly objected to the parts of the program centered on sex and draft resistance as anti-American, anti-law, and immoral. They were so out of line with the regular curriculum, plaintiffs alleged, that the substitution constituted a breach of contract. The court decided to the contrary and refused to interfere on several grounds. The one of most interest is that control of the curriculum was at the discretion of the college president. "Plaintiffs," said the court, "have no more right to choose the contents or formats of their classes than they would have to hire or fire faculty or select the textbooks for their classmates."

Accreditation

Few aspects of American higher education have been more characteristic than the variety of forms it has taken. This diversity has raised the persistent question of how the public is to know which forms really deserve to be called higher education. The State of New York was early to enact statutes which protected the public by establishing minimum standards for new institutions and requiring permission of the regents for use of the title of either college or university. But how could those already in existence be evaluated? The

[3] Not reported (1969).

federal government began but soon abandoned this task, and professional and regional associations stepped in to fill the vacuum. So effectively did they do so and so powerful did they become that it is not surprising that a few disappointed applicants for accreditation challenged the limits of the power of these agencies.

The first case of note was that of the State of North Dakota v. North Central Association of Colleges and Secondary Schools.[4] In this quarrel the state sought to prevent the association from withdrawing its accreditation from the State Agricultural College because of alleged irregularities in faculty dismissals. The governor of the state was much upset because he thought the association, a private agency, was interfering with the state direction of its public school system and that it was doing so unreasonably and without a fair hearing. Defendant met this objection by asserting that it was a voluntary association to which North Dakota could belong or not, as it saw fit, but if it wanted to retain membership it would have to abide by the rules. Besides, according to these rules defendant insisted plaintiff had not exhausted all recourse within the association before coming to court.

Finding nothing unreasonable in defendant's action, and also that plaintiff had not tried all remedies within the association, the judge came to the main point of interest:

> *Voluntary associations have the right to make their own regulations as to admission or expulsion of members and one who becomes a member, by its membership, assents to the constitution and rules of procedure adopted by such an association. The constitution, by-laws, and rules, knowingly assented to, become in effect a civil contract between the parties, whereby their rights are fixed and measured. Consequently, in the absence of fraud, collusion, arbitrariness, or breach of contract, such as give rise to a civil action, the decisions of such voluntary associations must be accepted . . . as conclusive.*
>
> *In churches, lodges, and all other like voluntary associations each person, on becoming a member, either by express*

[4] 23 Fed. Supp. 694 (1938).

107

stipulation or by implication, agrees to abide by all rules and regulations adopted by the organization, and courts will not interfere to control the enforcement of by-laws of such associations but will leave them free to enforce their own rules and regulations by such means and with such penalties as they may see proper to adopt for their own government. . . . Consequently such an organization is the judge of its own members, and membership therein is a privilege which may be accorded or withheld and not a right which can be gained independently and enforced. In the absence of breach of the law a [court] is powerless to compel admission . . . into such an association and if one's application is refused, it is equally without power to grant relief. . . . The rules laid down for the government of the members of an association form the measure of their rights in the premises; it is vain to appeal to a constitutional bill of rights, for such bills of rights are intended to protect the citizen against oppression by the government, not to afford protection against one's own agreements.

In the next case, Parsons College v. North Central Association,[5] a private rather than a public institution sought to avoid withdrawal of accreditation. The association sent one of its commissions to inspect the college's unconventional academic program. Finding that the college did not come up to standards, the commission notified it of its intent to withdraw accreditation. The school, profiting by the lesson of the North Dakota case, first appealed the report to the association's board of directors. After the appeal brought no change, the college turned to the courts for relief on the grounds that its accreditation had been withdrawn without due process and that the commission's report was arbitrary.

Addressing itself to these points the court granted no relief to the plaintiff.

Invoking a claim of due process, the college draws no support from the commands of the federal Constitution, as

[5] 271 Fed. Supp. 65 (1967).

contained in either the Fifth or Fourteenth Amendment. By their terms, these Constitutional guarantees control only the action of government. Designed to guard the individual against the . . . power of the state, they do not control the voluntary arrangements or relations of private citizens in their private dealings with each other. Here there is no suggestion that the association is an arm of government, making its acts the action of the state. With a corporate charter granted under general law, the association stands on the same footing as any private corporation organized for profit or not. The fact that the acts of the association in granting or denying accreditation may have some effect under governmental programs of assistance to students or colleges does not subject it to the Constitutional limits applicable to government, any more than a private employer whose decision to hire or fire may affect the employee's eligibility for governmental unemployment compensation. . . .

In its attack on standards, claiming them to be nebulous, the college relies upon decisions holding statutes to be unconstitutional on the ground that they are so vague as to be unintelligible to men of ordinary intelligence. The authority is inapposite. The standards of accreditation are not guides for the layman but for professionals in the field of education. Definiteness may prove, in another view, to be arbitrariness. The association was entitled to make a conscious choice in favor of flexible standards to accommodate variation in purpose and character among its constituent institutions, and to avoid forcing all into a rigid and uniform mold. No inference of undue vagueness can be drawn from the fact that the different committees of equally eminent educators disagreed in their recommendations. Courts have indeed been known to disagree in the application of the Constitution. . . .

The College questions the adequacy of the reasons given for withdrawing its accreditation. In this field, the courts are traditionally even more hesitant to intervene. The public benefits of accreditation, dispensing information and exposing misrepresentation, would not be enhanced by judicial intru-

109

sion. Evaluation by the peers of the college, enabled by experience to make comparative judgments, will best serve the paramount interest in the highest practicable standards in higher education. The price for such benefits is inevitably some injury to those who do not meet the measure, and some risk of conservatism produced by appraisals against a standard of what has already proven valuable in education. The association has achieved its power through the respect it has engendered through its work. If it fails to satisfy its members, they are free to join another group.

The most severe test of accreditation came in Marjorie Webster Junior College v. Middle States Accrediting Association.[6] The association, like the North Central Association in the preceding cases, was a private, voluntary association whose members were composed almost entirely of nonprofit institutions whose governing boards represented the public interest. Plaintiff, on the other hand, was a proprietary institution run for the profit of the Webster family, which owned all its stock and occupied most of its important administrative positions. When the college applied for accreditation the association refused even to inspect it because it was proprietary. The school then complained that the refusal to inspect it made more difficult the transfer of its graduates' credits to other institutions of higher education. Indeed, because of this difficulty it claimed that the association was a combination restraining the college's trade and therefore illegal under the Sherman Anti-Trust Act. The college went further and insisted that, because the association's standardizing function was so pervasive, it was governmental in character and therefore its discrimination was arbitrary, unreasonable, and contrary to due process. The association countered that higher education was not a business within the meaning of the Sherman Act, and that it was a private, voluntary association whose rules of membership were not subject to court review.

The lower court sided with the plaintiff and directed defend-

---

[6] This 1970 federal case had not been published officially by the time of the printing of this book.

110

ant to at least inspect the school and, if found qualified, to accredit it, admitting it into membership. The judge based his decision largely on a series of precedents in medical practice. Not only was medical practice held to be a business, but it was further established that if an otherwise qualified physician needed to belong to some professional organization in order to carry on his calling or business, that organization could not exclude him for arbitrary reasons. Reasoning analogously, the judge held that higher education was a business wherein membership in defendant association was necessary in carrying on plaintiff's business, that defendant's discrimination against plaintiff caused the college irreparable harm, and that this discrimination, based solely on plaintiff's not having a governing board responsible to the public interest, was arbitrary and unreasonable. An institution should be judged by its results, not its kind of governing board or whether it makes a profit.

This decision ran shivers down the spines of many accrediting associations. It is not surprising, therefore, that, when it was appealed, over a dozen briefs *amicus curiae* were filed. To the relief of the associations the appellate court reversed the lower court on nearly all points, declaring,

> *Appellee strongly urges, and the court below concluded, that once it be determined that appellee is engaging in "trade," restraint of that "trade" by appellant's conduct is subject to the limitations of the Sherman Act. If this were the ordinary case of a trade association alleged to have transgressed the bounds of reasonable regulation designed to mitigate the evils afflicting a particular industry, this reasoning might be conclusive. But in our view, the character of the defendant association, and the nature of the activities that it regulates, require a finer analysis.*
>
> *Despite the broad wording of the Sherman Act, it has long been settled that not every form of combination or conspiracy that restrains trade falls within its ambit. For the language of the act, although broad, is also vague, and in consequence of that vagueness, "perhaps not uncalculated," the*

courts have been left to give content to the statute, and in the performance of that function it is appropriate that courts should interpret its word in light of its legislative history and of the particular evils at which the legislation was aimed. . . .

The proscriptions of the Sherman Act were "tailored . . . for the business world," not for the noncommercial aspects of the liberal arts and the learned professions. In these contexts an incidental restraint of trade, absent an intent or purpose to affect the commercial aspects of the profession, is not sufficient to warrant application of the antitrust laws.

We are fortified in this conclusion by the historic reluctance of Congress to exercise control in educational matters. . . .

The increasing importance of private associations in the affairs of individuals and organizations has led to substantial expansion of judicial control over "The Internal Affairs of Associations not for Profit." Where membership in, or certification by, such an association is a virtual prerequisite to the practice of a given profession, courts have scrutinized the standards and procedures employed by the association notwithstanding their recognition of the fact that professional societies possess a specialized competence in evaluating the qualifications of an individual to engage in professional activities. . . .

Accordingly, we believe that judicial review of [the association's] standards should accord substantial deference to [the association's] judgment regarding the ends that it serves and the means most appropriate to those ends. Accreditation, . . . is as involved with educational philosophy as with yardsticks to measure the quality of education provided. . . . We do not think it has been shown to be unreasonable for [the association] to conclude that the desire for personal profit might influence educational goals in subtle ways difficult to detect but destructive, in the long run, of that atmosphere of academic inquiry which, perhaps even more than any quantitative measure of educational quality. [the association's] stan-

112

Academic Program

dards for accreditation seek to foster. Likewise, we may recognize that, even in nonprofit institutions, the battle for academic freedom and control of educational policy is still sporadically waged; but this factor would seem to strengthen, rather than weaken, the reasonableness of [the association's] judgment that motives of personal profit should not be allowed to influence the outcome. Finally, we need not say that [the association's] views of the proper measure for accreditation of an educational institution are the only, the best, or even particularly well chosen ones. The core of [its] argument is not that proprietary institutions are unworthy of accreditation, but rather that they, like many trade and professional schools, should properly be measured by standards different from those used by [the association], and which [it] is possessed of no special competence or experience in using. . . . [The college], however, is free to join with other proprietary institutions in setting up an association for the accreditation of institutions of such character; and such an association, if recognized, could obtain for its members all the benefits of accreditation by appellant save, perhaps, prestige.

Copyright

Professors have long been confronted with the peril of publish or perish. When they do publish they are confronted with a new peril in those who would unblushingly reproduce their materials for personal advantage and profit. Copyright law is designed to protect against this danger. Most professors, however, do not realize that there was copyright protection at common law before there was a copyright statute and that it applies to his oral as well as his recorded remarks. Williams v. Weisser[7] arose when defendant had an agent attend plaintiff's classes at the University of California at Los Angeles and take notes on his lectures, which were based on materials gained through scholarly inquiry. These notes were then typed, imprinted with a copyright, and offered for sale by Weisser who admitted a substantial similarity between the notes and the

[7] 78 Cal. Reptr. 542 (1969).

113

lectures. Friction over this practice developed not only between the professor and Weisser but also between Weisser and the university administration, which issued a memorandum on the matter to all members of the faculty. When Weisser continued this practice in spite of the memorandum, the professor sued in order to prohibit the further publication of his lectures. The court not only granted the injunction but also awarded plaintiff fifteen hundred dollars for damages. The lower court made this award proceeding on the theory that defendant had infringed plaintiff's common law copyright and that he had invaded plaintiff's privacy by placing the professor's name on the notes sold.

Defendant set forth several grounds as the basis for an appeal to a higher court. If anyone owned a copyright to plaintiff's lectures, he first asserted, it was UCLA. Plaintiff was an employee, according to him, whose product belonged to his employer. By lecturing, defendant next asserted, plaintiff placed his materials in the public domain and therefore divested himself of any copyright he may have had. Finally, the publication of the notes was a fair use which in no way was an abuse of plaintiff's personality or reputation, especially since, as defendant alleged, the notes were not original, being just an embellished commentary on the work of others already in the public domain.

After searching and explicating both English and American precedents the appeal court found no support for defendant's contentions. Disposing of them in order it had this to say:

> *Defendant also claims that plaintiff is in the position of an employee for hire whose employment calls for the creation of a copyrightable work, or, perhaps, of an independent contractor who has been so commissioned. . . . In such cases it is usually presumed that, unless a different intention is shown, the employer or commissioner is the owner of the copyright. . . .*
>
> *This contention calls for some understanding of the purpose for which a university hires a professor and what rights it may reasonably expect to retain after the services have been rendered. A university's obligation to its students is to*

114

make the subject matter covered by a course available for study by various methods, including classroom presentation. It is not obligated to present the subject by means of any particular expression. As far as the teacher is concerned, neither the record in this case nor any custom known to us suggests that the university can prescribe his way of expressing the ideas he puts before his students. Yet expression is what this lawsuit is all about. No reason has been suggested why a university would want to retain the ownership of a professor's expression. Such retention would be useless except possibly for making a little profit from a publication and for making it difficult for the teacher to give the same lectures, should he change jobs.

Indeed the undesirable consequences which would follow from a holding that a university owns the copyright to the lectures of its professors are such as to compel a holding that it does not. Professors are a peripatetic lot, moving from campus to campus. The courses they teach begin to take shape at one institution and are developed and embellished at another. That, as a matter of fact, was the case here. Plaintiff testified that the notes on which his lectures were based were derived from a similar course which he had given at another university. If defendant is correct, there must be some rights of that school which were infringed at UCLA. Further, should plaintiff leave UCLA and give a substantially similar course at his next post, UCLA would be able to enjoin him from using the material, which according to defendant, it owns.

The oral delivery of the lectures did not divest plaintiff of his common law copyright to his lectures. Nothing tangible was delivered to the students and every case that has considered the problem of divestment from the limited versus general publication point of view has reached the conclusion that the giving of a lecture is not a general publication. . . . "The persons present at a lecture are not the general public, but a limited class of the public . . . admitted for the sole . . . purpose of receiving individual instruction; they may make any use they can of the lecture, to the extent of taking it down

115

*in shorthand, for their own information and improvement, but
cannot publish it." . . .*

*An author who owns the common law copyright to his
work can determine whether he wants to publish it and, if so,
under what circumstances. Plaintiff had prepared his notes
for a specific purpose—as an outline for lectures to be delivered to a class of students. Though he apparently considered
them adequate for that purpose, he did not desire a commercial distribution with which his name was associated. Right or
wrong, he felt that his professional standing could be jeop-
ardized.*

Macmillan Company v. King[8] arose where the professor's
remarks had already been published, the more frequent instance of
copyright infringement. Defendant was an instructor who used one
of the books published by the professor as a text. He recommended
that his students purchase it but could not control whether they did
or not. His method of instruction involved making memoranda and
outlines which closely followed the text, and distributing these to
his students with the distinct understanding that they be returned
to him after use. Under no circumstances did he sell or lease his
prepared materials. Nevertheless plaintiff sued for a restriction
against him because his materials were versions of a copyrighted
book within the prohibition of the copyright act.

Said the court, upholding the publisher's side of the lawsuit,

*It seems to me that the defendant's method of dealing
with the book has resulted in an appropriation by him of the
author's ideas and language more extensive than the copyright
law permits. It is true that the whole book has not been thus
dealt with, but the copyright protects every substantial component part of the book, as well as the whole. Although the
reproduction of the author's ideas and language is . . . frag-
mentary, and frequently presents them in somewhat distorted
form, important portions of them are left substantially recog-
nizable. . . . I [do not] see any reason to doubt that . . .*

[8] 223 Fed. 62 (1914).

116

these "outlines" might readily "cause the student to think he [could] meet the minimum requirements without using the book itself." It cannot be said that the outlines go no further than to "give just enough information to put the reader upon inquiry" regarding the contents of the book. . . .

I must hold that the defendant's sheets are not . . . such abridgments from the copyrighted book as he has the right to make, and that they constitute versions *of substantial portions of the book, such as the plaintiff alone has the right to make. . . .*

Printing *I must regard as including typewriting or mimeographing, for the purposes of the act, and he has therefore printed them. Can he be said to have* published *them . . . in such sense as to make his publication an infringement, entitling the plaintiff to an injunction? . . .*

It is not necessary, in order to constitute publication, that they should have been offered in the market to whoever chose to buy them. There may be a limited publication, which will entitle the owner of the copyright to an injunction. . . . Although the defendant issued the infringing sheets only to his own pupils, and to them only upon agreement that they should be returned to him within a limited time, the evidence . . . shows either that the agreement was not fulfilled in every case, or that these sheets were copied before being returned. No precautions against such copying appear to have been taken. I must hold that sufficient publication . . . has been shown to constitute infringement.

If the above conclusions are right, I am unable to believe that the defendant's use of the outlines is any the less infringement of the copyright because he is a teacher, because he uses them in teaching the contents of the book, because he might lecture upon the contents of the book without infringing, or because his pupils might have taken their own notes of his lectures without infringing. . . .

The evidence can hardly be said to show that the infringing outlines have injured the sale of the book. Nothing more appears than that they might do so, by enabling students to get along without the book who otherwise would have had to buy it. . . . Proof of actual damage is not necessary for the issuance of an injunction, if infringement appears and damage may probably follow from its continuance.

This case, decided before the First World War, carries increased significance today when mechanical copiers have been greatly improved and when much greater use of original as well as textbook materials is being made in higher education. The copier enables the professor to make materials from widely scattered sources quickly and easily available for his whole class. It seems one must weigh the interests of the author and publisher on the one hand and the interests of the classroom instructor on the other. Perhaps a new definition is needed of the fair use of published materials.

Counseling

Helping the student thread his way through the maze of technical scholastic requirements, to say nothing of the maze of his personal problems on campus, has become a very complex operation in modern higher education. Indeed, so complex has it become that trained personnel experts in guidance and counseling have developed to meet the student need. Success in this undertaking depends to a high degree on mutual confidence between the student and the counselor. Satisfactory fulfillment of this confidential relationship has raised legal as well as professional problems. The following four cases sample widely different aspects of the field.

Bank v. Board of Higher Education[9] records the disappointment of a plaintiff who had been notified to present himself for graduation ceremonies and whose friends and relatives had assembled for the occasion only to learn that his name was omitted from the commencement program. Worse yet, the omission was not a typographical error. His bachelor's degree was withheld because, unbeknownst to him and his advisor, he had not satisfied all the requirements for the degree. He had taken two courses without being in residence or attending classes, which was contrary to Brook-

9 273 N.Y.S. 2nd 796 (1966).

lyn College regulations. The origin of the student's embarrassment was not difficult to unravel. Brooklyn College afforded its seniors an optional program whereby they could substitute a year of full-time study in an approved law school for a year at the college. The student obtained approval to attend Syracuse University Law School but his attendance there was complicated by the fact that he still lacked two courses to complete his undergraduate major in psychology. According to routine he sought advice from his dean who referred him to the office of guidance and counseling which sent him to the chairman of the psychology department. The advice he got there was that he could take these courses without attending class, providing he got the consent of the instructors involved. Both consented, informing him of the materials that needed to be read, so the student registered, did the reading, took the examinations, and passed the courses. Apparently none of his advisors knew, as the president of the college testified at the trial, that there was a college policy against this practice.

Not being personally at fault, plaintiff asked the court to order defendant to confer the bachelor's degree on him. In directing that this be done, the court observed,

> *The authority of the dean of faculty ultimately to determine the acceptability of a program for the awarding of an A.B. degree is unquestioned. This authority, however, is not absolute. . . .*
>
> *The dean of faculty may not escape the binding effect of the acts of his agents performed within the scope of their apparent authority, and the consequences that must equitably follow therefrom. Having given permission to take the subject courses in the manner prescribed, through his agents, . . . he cannot in the circumstances later assert that the courses should have been taken in some other manner.*

Fortunately in the Bank case there was a happy ending. Not so in Bogus v. Iverson.[10] Defendant was a college counselor for personal, vocational, educational, and other student problems.

[10] 10 Wis. 2nd 129—102 N.E. 2nd 228 (1960).

119

In the course of his duties he counseled plaintiffs' daughter, who was emotionally disturbed. After five months of counseling he suggested its termination, and six weeks later the girl committed suicide. The parents claimed the counselor was responsible for the death because he failed to secure emergency psychiatric treatment and also failed to notify them of their daughter's condition. The counselor admitted the facts but denied they rendered him legally liable for the death. The trial court agreed: "To hold that a teacher who has had no training, education, or experience in medical fields is required to recognize in a student a condition the diagnosis of which is in a specialized and technical medical field, would require a duty beyond reason." The appellate court also agreed, stating further,

Plaintiffs allege defendant was charged with the maintenance of a counseling and testing center for various educational, vocational, and personal problems which students of the college might have, but that fact does not qualify him as an expert in the field of medicine or psychiatry. Granting that he had some knowledge of Jeannie's emotional and other difficulties as the result of his meetings with her, during a period of five months, as a teacher he cannot be charged with the same degree of care based on such knowledge as a person trained in medicine or psychiatry could exercise.

The first act of negligence alleged is that the defendant failed to secure psychiatric treatment for Jeannie "after he was aware or should have been aware of her inability to care for the safety of herself." This clearly implies that he should have known she had suicidal tendencies. But there is no allegation of fact that would have apprised the defendant, as a reasonably prudent man, that she had such tendencies. The statement is merely a conclusion. The same comment applies to the second act of negligence alleged, that of failing to advise the parents, "thus preventing them from securing proper medical care for her." The duty of advising her parents could arise only from facts establishing knowledge on the part of defendant of a mental or emotional state which required medical care; and no such facts are alleged.

120

Academic Program

The allegation that defendant failed to provide proper student guidance apparently refers to the fact that he "suggested termination of future interviews regarding her problems." . . .

There is no allegation that the interviews between the defendant and Jeannie benefited her or that there was a duty on his part to continue them or that their termination caused the injury or placed her in a worse position than she was when they were begun.

Even with this disposition of the case the question still arises, could the defendant have reasonably foreseen his handling of the case as the proximate cause of the girl's suicide? On the point of causation the court had this to say:

A proximate cause is one in which is involved the idea of necessity. . . . A remote cause is one which is inconclusive in reasoning, because from it no certain conclusion can be legitimately drawn. In other words, a remote cause is a cause the connection between which and the effect is uncertain, vague, or indeterminate. . . . The proximate cause being given, the effect must follow. . . . The remote cause being given, the effect may or may not follow.

As a general rule a person will not be relieved of liability by an intervening force which could reasonably have been foreseen, nor by one which is a normal incident of the risk created. However, if such intervening force takes the form of suicide the practically unanimous rule is that such act is a new and independent agency which does not come within and complete a line of causation from the wrongful act to the death and therefore does not render defendant liable for the suicide.

One intricate point which frequently arises in counseling concerns access to college and university records on the student. In Morris v. Smiley[11] the plaintiff sued the dean of student life at the University of Texas to let him inspect and copy records kept by the

[11] 378 S.W. 2nd 149 (1964).

121

dean relating to plaintiff. Permission turned on whether the records kept by the dean were public, and the court's decision is principally interesting for its definition of what are public records.

It is said that a public record is one required by law to be kept . . . to serve as a memorial and evidence of something written, said, or done, . . . but this is not quite inclusive of all that may properly be considered public records. For whenever a written record of the transactions of a public officer in his office is [an] . . . appropriate mode of discharging the duties of his office, it is not only his right, but his duty, to keep that memorial whether expressly required to do so or not; and when kept it becomes a public document which belongs to the office rather than to the officer.

Closely akin to the question of public records is the question of whether communications of a counsellor are privileged. In Kenney v. Gurley,[12] a student was sent home from Tuskegee Institute because she was suffering from a venereal infection. The medical director wrote Velma's mother a letter informing her of the circumstances. The dean also wrote the mother a letter in which she refused the girl permission to return to the college because her condition "seems to indicate that Velma has not been living right." The mother and daughter considered the remark libellous and sued to recover damages. Defendant pleaded that since her letter bore no malice against the student, it was to be considered a privileged communication. The trial court awarded damages but the appeal court ordered a new trial, stating, "[A] personal, authoritative letter addressed . . . and sent to the parent or guardian of a dismissed student [relating the] reason for the student's dismissal or for the denial of readmission is a privileged occasion. Whereas here, the evidence descriptive of the occasion is undisputed, the inquiry whether the occasion was privileged is a question of law to be decided by the court, not by the jury."

[12] 208 Ala. 623—95 S. 34 (1923).

FIVE

Torts

Incidental to Instruction

The law has long maintained, and still does in some jurisdictions, that public institutions of higher learning and those privately endowed were not liable for damages or injuries to their students or other beneficiaries. The tuition and other charges of such institutions were so much lower than the true cost of services performed that students enjoyed a sizeable subsidy. It did not become them, therefore, as beneficiaries of a charity to hold it responsible for its torts. The funds of such institutions were held in trust to be devoted toward their charitable ends and consequently were not to be diverted to pay damages for wrongs or torts committed by those who administer them.

Recently, however, this rule has been changing. Its new statement starts with the premise that for negligent conduct liability rather than immunity is the rule. Reparation for a wrong done is no longer to be withheld from an injured party because he did not pay in full or was not bound to pay for the activity out of which the injury arose. One who undertakes to benefit another must do so with due care. Charity is long-suffering and kind but at common law it cannot be careless. The fear that charities will not survive if they must answer in damages for their wrongs is no longer entertained. Such damages may add to their operating expenses but they can be guarded against by carrying insurance.

The cases which have

arisen against this background in college and university are abundant, and only a few can be noted. A leading case among those growing out of the academic program is Hamburger v. Cornell University.[1] A coed, the plaintiff, was performing a prescribed experiment in the chemistry laboratory. Due to a wrong selection of ingredients an explosion occurred, seriously injuring her. She sought to hold the university responsible for her injuries but it claimed that she was responsible for picking up the wrong ingredients from a supply table. Her view was that the university's agent gave her the wrong ingredients from the supply room. Since there was no evidence of mislabelling of the ingredients, the trial judge did not charge the jury on this point, but he did ask them to decide whether the school had been negligent in not subjecting the ingredients to prior analysis and in the selection of the agent involved in the accident. Whereas the trial court found for the plaintiff, the intermediate court of appeal found for the defendant. The final court of appeal also sided with the defendant:

> *We think a hospital's immunity from liability for the errors of surgeons and physicians is matched in the case of a university by a like immunity from liability for the errors of professors or instructors or other members of its staff of teachers. . . . There is indeed a duty to select them with due care. That duty fulfilled, there is none to supervise day by day the details of their teaching. The governing body of a university makes no attempt to control its professors and instructors as if they were its servants. By practice and tradition, the members of the faculty are masters, and not servants, in the conduct of the classroom. They have the independence appropriate to a company of scholars. . . . The members of the defendant's staff of teachers were not charged with any duty in respect of the general care of chemicals held in the main storeroom as permanent sources of supply. They were professors or instructors, not curators or custodians, if the distinction be important. . . . We think the consequences of their negligence in the*

[1] 240 N.Y. 328—148 N.E. 539 (1925).

124

fulfillment of the duties incidental to the teaching function may not be charged to the defendant.

We find no evidence that anyone in the service of the defendant, whether instructor or mere employee, had been carelessly selected.

Jay v. Walla Walla College[2] was another case growing out of an accident in a chemistry laboratory. While plaintiff was conducting an experiment in his laboratory he heard an explosion across the hall. Running to see what had happened, he found two students trying to extinguish a fire. He seized a fire extinguisher to help them, but found it empty. Just then an even more severe explosion occurred causing plaintiff injuries for which he wanted to recover damages. The college tried to avoid liability by claiming that the student was contributorily negligent because he went to the scene of the accident of his own volititon and therefore any untoward consequences were his fault rather than the college's. The court did not see it that way:

Appellant contends that respondent both knew of and appreciated the danger. The general rule is that when a person voluntarily assents to a known danger, he must abide the consequences, even if another party is negligent. . . . But a party is excused from the force of the rule if an emergency is found to exist or if the life or property of another is in peril. . . .

A person who, without negligence on his part, is suddenly and unexpectedly confronted with peril . . . is not expected nor required to use the same . . . prudence that is required . . . in calmer and more deliberate moments. His duty is to exercise only the care that an ordinarily prudent person would exercise in the same situation. If at that moment he does what appears to him to be the best thing to do, . . . he does all the law requires of him, although in the light of after-events it should appear that a different course would have been better.

[2] 53 Wash. 2nd 590—335 P. 2nd 458 (1959).

The Courts and Higher Education

The role of the instructor can be critical in these tort cases. Take Brittan v. State[3] as an instance. A coed was taking a physical fitness test under the direction of a senior physical education student who, after some instruction in administering the test, was giving it for the first time. The instructor himself was not present. During the test the student snapped a ligament through overexertion, which resulted in a permanent injury. Stating that she should recover damages, the court observed,

> *The State of New York, through its agents, the staff of Cortland State Teachers College, owed to the claimant the duty of reasonable care in the conduct of the tests to which she was required to submit. . . . That duty embraced the proper administration and supervision of these tests. An adequate degree of supervision is provided by furnishing an experienced and competent man. . . . It is extremely doubtful that the claimant received proper instructions . . . on how to take the test. She was not instructed to do any warm up exercises prior to taking the test, a procedure recommended by the experts.*
>
> *Allowing a physical education class to be conducted by a student physical education instructor in the absence of a qualified instructor has been held to constitute negligence.*

Incidental to Athletics

One of the places where injuries occur most frequently in higher education is in athletic contests. In Kaufman v. City of New York[4] the athletic arena was a basketball court. Plaintiff's son was involved in a basketball game, in the course of which he and a member of the opposite team jumped for the ball simultaneously. In doing so they struck heads with such concussion that the son immediately became unconscious and subsequently died. The father sued the city, claiming that it was negligent in not providing supervision for the game. However, he got no comfort from the court:

[3] 103 N.Y.S. 2nd 485 (1951).
[4] 124 N.Y.S. 767 (1961).

126

There is no contention . . . of improper construction of the gymnasium, or that the premises were otherwise maintained in an unsafe or improper condition. The sole complaint is the alleged failure to properly supervise the playing of this three-man basketball game.

Even if it be assumed that there were no instructors present at the time, . . . there is no legal causal connection between the alleged failure of an instructor to be present and the injury and consequent death of the decedent.

If the instructor were present and watching and supervising the game, he could not have stopped the boys from bumping their heads together; that is one of the natural and normal possible consequences or occurrences in a game of this sort which cannot be prevented no matter how adequate the supervision. . . .

If it may be said that the absence of a supervisor or instructor, under the circumstances, was negligence, still such lack of supervision was not the proximate cause of the accident.

Therefore, assuming that there was here the absence of a supervisor or instructor and that such absence constituted negligence, still, under the circumstances, such lack of supervision was not the proximate cause of the accident.

Football was the game from which University of Denver v. Nemeth[5] arose. For the injury he suffered in the game the student put in a claim for benefits under the workmen's compensation act. Whether he should receive the benefits turned not so much on the injury as on whether his presence on the university's team made him an employee. The university paid him fifty dollars a month for various odd jobs about the campus, but since the injury in question did not grow out of this employment the school insisted no compensation was due. The athlete, however, stated that he was told by those in authority at the university that getting a job "would be decided on the football field." Indeed, after several weeks of practice he was awarded the job. In addition, the football coach testi-

[5] 127 Colo. 385—257 P. 2nd 423 (1953).

fied that a job ceased if a student was cut from the football squad. On this evidence the court sustained the award of compensation, holding that playing football was incidental to his employment:

> *The employment at the university, so far as Nemeth was concerned, was dependent on his playing football, and he could not retain his job without playing football. The evidence before the Industrial Commission was to the effect that his job . . . came to an end when he ceased to "make good" in football. . . . The commission and the district court . . . properly concluded . . . that Nemeth was an employee of the university and sustained an accidental injury arising out of and in the course of his employment.*

There is an implicit inference in the court's opinion, though the court stopped short of making it explicit, that the student was a hired athlete. It is an interesting speculation whether, if he had been paid exclusively to play football, he would have received compensation. An athletic scholarship might be viewed not as employment but as casual assistance to help a student obtain his college education. Indeed, the University of Denver tried to convince the court that his work about the campus was not employment but just this sort of casual help. The university was alarmed at what awarding the athlete compensation might mean for hundreds of students to whom it paid small emoluments for odd jobs to defray their college expenses.

Unfair Use of Name

Not all tort cases arise from negligence or personal injury. In Cornell v. Messing Bakeries[6] the alleged harm was the use of the university's name in advertising the bakery's product. The facts in the case are unusual. A professor at the university had developed a formula for baking bread which was highly nutritious, and the formula was released to the public without restriction of its commercial use. The bakery made extensive investment in producing and promoting bread baked according to this formula. It advertised

[6] 138 N.Y.S. 2nd 280 (1955).

its product as Cornell Bread, using a red pennant with white letters, the official colors of the university. Cornell took exception and in correspondence with the bakery tried to prescribe the use of its name.

> *The memorandum stated that any baker might use the phrase Cornell Formula Bread in letters not more than one-half inch high, printed on both sides of the wrapper, if the wrapper also contained the name of the baker "in larger letters" and as a "more prominent feature of the wrapper" than the phrase containing "Cornell"; if both the formula and a disclaimer of university connection also be printed; and if "no pennants, flags, or other devices or symbols or words indicative of a college or university except as above authorized" be used.*

The bakery thought these restrictions were unfairly burdensome and only conformed to them in part. Consequently the university brought suit to prohibit the use of its name except under the conditions stipulated. The lower court substantially granted the request which, with slight modifications, was sustained on appeal:

> *We have no difficulty in holding to be valid Cornell's argument that it has a legal interest in preventing the exploitation of its name for business purposes. It is not necessary . . . that plaintiff be another business in the same line. . . . The ground of equitable intervention is not merely "unfair competition" in the limited sense of protecting the solidly acquired rights of one business enterprise against another striving for the same market. Equity may also shield the thrust by business into the kind of legal rights acquired in areas entirely removed from commercial activities. . . .*
>
> *The theory underlying injunctive interference is that an educational institution which has won large public prestige by hard effort and at high cost ought not, against its will, have that prestige diluted by a commercial use of its name, suggesting connection or benefit to the institution from the enterprise.*
>
> *The key word in the name of the university might, of*

course, be used under circumstances which would not touch upon or invade the university's area of protection. A coal mine or a tug or trucking enterprise might, for example, use Cornell *and no one would think the university either involved or concerned. But there are many other kinds of use of the main component word of the university name which could be read to suggest a link to the university; and Cornell Recipe Bread using a formula worked out at the university could quite sensibly be regarded as unduly and adversely affecting the university's rights when commercially exploited.*

The question would, as we see it, often be an open one of the facts, and so we regard it in this case. Because this bread formula did come from Cornell University; because of the general publication of the findings in trade and other journals on their promulgation at the university; because of the conjunctive use of recipe *or* formula *with* Cornell *and with* bread, *the use of* Cornell *here may be seen not just as coincidence but as having a pointed reference to the plaintiff.*

Whereas Cornell was more or less successful in protecting its name, another well-known university was not. In Notre Dame v. Twentieth Century-Fox,[7] the dispute grew out of the release of the motion picture *John Goldfarb, Please Go Home,* based on a book of the same title. The university took offense because the farcical movie appropriated and exploited for trade purposes its name, symbols, and reputation, and because by involving the president of Notre Dame it invaded his privacy.

The lower court awarded plaintiff protection against this use of its name, but an intermediate appellate court reversed the decision and pinpointed the issue by asking, "Is there any basis for an inference on the part of rational readers or viewers that the antics engaging their attention are anything more than fictional or that the real Notre Dame is in some way associated with its fabrication?" Answering its own question the court said emphatically "none whatever."

[7] 256 N.Y.S. 301 (1965).

Defendants argue that injunctive relief would violate the First Amendment, but that is an issue we do not reach. It is permissible to express praise or derision of a college's athletic activities in a journal of news or opinion. If such a journal, a novel, and a photoplay are on a parity in law as media of expression, extension of the doctrine of unfair competition to interdict praise or derision by means of the novel or the photoplay would seem without justification. Social cost may properly be considered in these matters . . . and the granting of an injunction in this case would outlaw large areas heretofore deemed permissible subject matter for literature and the arts.

A majority of the New York Court of Appeals without opinion affirmed this ruling but nevertheless two of its judges joined in a vigorous dissent.[8]

The argument is made, and this appears to be the main thrust of the opinion in the appellate division, that if we enjoin the release of this film it would preclude authors from telling tales of an institution, corporation or public figure without their consent. This is the real evil that the constitutional protection for free expression is aimed at. It is urged that a permanent injunction in the present case would muzzle criticism of our public institutions by authors of fiction. The cry goes up that an injunction here spells out the end of the lampoon, the satire—the right of free criticism and comment. But all these fears are unfounded since the facts of this case, revealed by the defendants and confirmed by the contents of the book and picture, do not serve as examples of opinion, information, education, or comment about a real institution. Rather, what is before this court is simply a fictional story with the name of a real institution affixed to it and the symbols used in it for the sake of capitalizing on the publicity value and reputation which the real institution has given those names and symbols.

[8] 15 N.Y. 2nd 940—207 N.E. 2nd 508 (1965).

The Courts and Higher Education

There is no attempt here to satirize the University of Notre Dame. If the authors had desired this effect they could have achieved it, as much as they achieved their satire of the State Department and the CIA. The admissions of the defendants in their affidavits make it clear that there is no attempt in this picture to satirize Notre Dame, or even depict that institution. The defendants have urged that as a matter of state law the usual rules of unfair competition, such as the rule in the Cornell case, ought not to be extended to the publication industry, which would include the motion picture industry. They say that to do so would place unreasonable limitations on the traditional institutions of comment, discussion, criticism, satire, ridicule, burlesque, and lampoonery. In fact it is these very institutions, integral parts of free expression, which are protected by the Constitution. We do not contend that these forms of expression should be fettered by unreasonable prior restraint. In fact we do not think that we need concern ourselves here with the amount of protection which ought to be given these institutions, for with regard to this case none of them are present. On the record before us the presence of the name and symbols of the University of Notre Dame in the scenario is not the result of an attempt to make a satire of it, or even to comment on it.

SIX

Overview

The foregoing cases have highlighted significant decisions of the courts with regard to higher education. Although, as stated at the outset, there has been no intent to be definitive in the selection of cases, it would be amiss to point out the tall trees without saying something about the forest of which they are a part. What on the whole, one might ask, has been the impact of the courts on colleges and universities? It is not easy to answer this question because the incidence of the impact has been shifting, especially since the middle of this century. Historically, universities have enjoyed a large degree of autonomy. Indeed, the university has been defined as a republic of scholars. To call it that makes considerable sense. Since scholars are experts in their various disciplines and since only experts are adequate judges of their own expertise, obviously they must enjoy autonomy in making decisions involving expertise. For this reason, no doubt, courts originally refrained from interfering in the internal administration of institutions of higher education. They examined the legal authority of the institution to perform an act but restrained from judging the propriety of the act itself. In the past quarter century, however, the courts have shown an increasing disposition to judge propriety too. Let us briefly review samples of the cases highlighted according to whether the court examined the authority to act or examined the propriety of an authorized act.

The preference for university autonomy is clear in Hartigan v. Board of Regents of the University of Virginia.[1] In that case, it will be remembered, a professor took exception to his dismissal because he received no notice of the proceedings against him and no opportunity to be heard in his own defense. Whether he was entitled to notice depended upon whether as a professor he was a public official. The court held he was not, that he had no authority in this capacity. But the court went further to indicate an emphatic distaste for recognizing a right to notice in any event because to do so would open the way for the court to arrogate to itself the prerogatives of the university governing board. It did not want to infringe on the autonomy of the university. This point of view is so critically important that it is well to quote again pertinent lines from the judge's opinion: "The proposition is asserted that every action of the regents may be made the subject of judicial review. . . . Under this theory the courts would control the board of regents, would paralyze the arm of the executive, deprive the executive of its power over the university, plainly conferred by the legislature. . . . I am ready to disclaim the assumption of this power, which I would consider little less than usurpation."

Giving this principle a constitutional foundation is Sterling v. Regents of the University of Michigan, which definitely established the autonomy of that state university. In that instance the legislature directed the regents to locate a school of homeopathic medicine in Detroit rather than Ann Arbor. The regents refused to comply, defying the state legislature. After a thorough analysis of the state constitution the court concluded that the university was not an arm of the legislature but was in fact constitutionally autonomous, a virtual fourth branch of government. Note that the court did not express an opinion on where as a matter of policy the medical school should be located but merely confined itself to deciding who had the authority to make the policy.

While dealing with the constitutional ground for the autonomy of the university we cannot ignore the Dartmouth College case, in which Chief Justice John Marshall thoroughly protected

[1] For references to decisions cited in this chapter, see the index.

134

the independence of existing private institutions of higher learning from take-over by the state. He did not overturn the New Hampshire decision to have a public university but maintained only that the state had no authority to unilaterally appropriate Dartmouth to its own ends. To have permitted the unilateral alteration of the Dartmouth Charter, Marshall contended, would have violated the constitutional prohibition against a state's abrogating the obligation of contracts. Perhaps the great chief justice would have taken a different view of the case under present circumstances. Today if an institution of higher learning derives substantial subsidies from the state—which from the time of its founding Dartmouth had from the State of New Hampshire—an instance of *state action* may be established which vests even private colleges with a public interest. Even so, courts today are in no hurry to find state action.

A further refinement of the principle of autonomy for expertise is found in the case of Marjorie Webster Junior College v. Middle States Accrediting Association.[2] This private association was composed of eleemosynary institutions, and refused to accredit or even to inspect the proprietary junior college. Since the college was unaccredited its graduates suffered in transferring their academic credits to other institutions, and it claimed that the association was a combination in restraint of trade under the Sherman Anti-Trust Act. The court held not only that higher education was not a business within the meaning of the Sherman Act but that eleemosynary and proprietary institutions differed so subtly in philosophy that it did not feel warranted in intervening in the affairs of the association.

A less important illustration of our thesis is to be found in another Michigan case already cited, Sittler v. Board of Control. The authority to employ was at issue. The head of a department had employed an instructor in a telephone conversation later confirmed in a letter. The instructor taught for a short while, after which his appointment was abruptly terminated. When he sued for breach of contract the court found that the college governing board,

[2] Cf. Z. Chafee, "Internal Affairs of Associations Not for Profit," *Harvard Law Review*, 1930, *43*, 1028, 1029.

not the department head, had the authority to make a contract. Note that the court did not invade the area of expertise ordinarily reserved to the faculty, that of determining its own membership—in this case of deciding whether this particular instructor should be added to their community of scholars. It merely stated that the apparent departmental authority to hire him did not exist.

A case in which the court was sorely tempted to replace professional academic judgment with its own is that of Lesser v. Board of Higher Education. In this case, to freshen memory, a young student graduated from high school with a scholastic average of 84.3, barely short of the 85 required for admission to the college of his choice. The lower court thought the high school authorities and the college admissions officer had exercised their discretion arbitrarily and unreasonably and directed the boy's admission. The intermediate court, however, did not think it arbitrary, taking the view that this was just the sort of delicate area of expertise which the court should refrain from entering.

To illustrate the same principle in an extracurricular rather than curriculum case, take Jones v. Vassar College. The college in that case had autonomously decided to go coeducational after many years as an exclusively girls' institution. The question of visiting hours for men in women's dormitories arose, and the faculty and administration in the fullness of their wisdom allowed the students to vote on this internal question of campus discipline. As might be expected, they opted for unlimited hours, much to the distress of the mother of one of the girls. Having sent her daughter to Vassar under restricted visiting rules, she thought the college had an implied obligation to continue them while her daughter was there. The court held that such a change in rules was well within the authority of the institution and refused to be alarmed at the discretion exercised by the college in putting the matter to a student vote.

If the foregoing cases do not prove our principle of noninterference with the expertise of the university certainly those just coming into the courts, but as yet unadjudicated, should. Some of these cases ask the court to close the university, others to open universities already closed. In some instances university officials have been sued for large sums of money because students claim they have been deprived of educational and political rights by campus disturbances which the officials allegedly condoned by failing to call in police. Implied in these cases is the premise that university officials have made unwise policy decisions which the courts can rectify. This premise is dubious and may well lead to the atrophy of the channels of the campus for conflict resolution.

Whether or not the courts deal with such cases the issues that generate them will surely persist. For it is clear that judicial intervention will not remove the problems that divide and disrupt campuses. It is equally clear that judicial abstinence will not bring peace to the campus. If the courts decline to intercede, responsibility for solving internal conflicts will revert to the campus, where it belongs. One last effort must be made to develop on-campus tribunals that can resolve issues which are now increasingly relegated to external forums. Rather than going to the courts, cannot campus problems be solved on campus with comparable integrity and vastly greater expertise? Of course, campus decisions may not always be obeyed. But neither may court orders, as the number of recent contempt proceedings suggests.[3]

In most of the cases reviewed so far, the court limited its decision to the grant of authority. In only one case did it pass on whether the authority to act had been wisely exercised. On the whole this self-imposed restriction seems quite appropriate. Judges are trained in the law, not in academic policy, and therefore should leave professional decisions to academic personnel.[4] Nevertheless, since the middle of this century courts have more and more been drawn into judging the propriety of decisions. The magnet attracting the courts into this area has been the Bill of Rights. The question they have been asked to decide is whether decisions hitherto

[3] R. M. O'Neil, "Judicial Overkill," *Change,* September–October, 1970, 41.

[4] N. Glazer, "Campus Rights and Responsibilities: A Role for Lawyers?" *American Scholar,* 1970, *39*, 445–462.

left to the expertise of the university are consistent with rights guaranteed by the First, Fourth, Fifth, and Fourteenth amendments. Insisting that academe meet the standards of these amendments has strengthened the autonomy of the university in some areas and shaken it in others.

The intervention of the courts in internal discretionary matters at the university has been most justified in the area of the First Amendment.[5] In spite of its guaranty of free speech it may startle some to learn that not until after the Second World War did anyone invoke court action to bring academic freedom under its protecting cloak. Previously, academic freedom for scholarly expertise was treated as a matter of institutional and internal administration. Too often under such a regime, however, professors were cowed and intimidated by autocratic presidents and trustees. To protect the exercise of their expertise professors sought a remedy in 1915, not by appeal to the courts but by forming the American Association of University Professors. The A.A.U.P. could blacklist offending institutions, yet it was powerless to make restitution to aggrieved professors. Finally, during the McCarthy era, in Sweezey v. New Hampshire, a threatened professor sought the protection of the First Amendment and won it in the United States Supreme Court. Almost everyone is agreed that this intervention on the campus, giving academic freedom constitutional status, has strengthened, not diminished, university autonomy. This case was later reinforced by Wieman v. Updegraff, in which scholarly expertise was shielded from loyalty oath legislation, and by Slochower v. Board of Higher Education, in which this expertise was shielded from adverse inference by a professor's pleading the Fifth Amendment.

Furthermore, First Amendment freedoms were extended to students as well as to faculty. In Dickey v. Alabama the editor of an undergraduate newspaper received protection, and in Antonelli v. Hammond a student editor was supported even though his columns carried allegedly obscene materials. Hammond v. South Carolina involved freedom of assembly by the students, and again

[5] W. P. Murphy, "Academic Freedom—An Emerging Constitutional Right," *Law and Contemporary Problems,* 1963, *28,* 447–486.

138

federal courts sheltered them from the chilling effect of prior restriction. Robust as we must expect the assertion of freedom of speech to be, the courts have not allowed violence, as in Grossner v. Columbia University, or obscenities, as in Goldberg v. University of California, to be a protected form of free speech on the campus. There was a time when these student cases would have been disposed of by faculty and administration without further review because the college or university stood *in loco parentis*. No longer. But on the other hand, the autonomy of the university now has been enlarged by the courts to include the academic freedom of the students as well as the academic freedom of the professors.

The impact of intervention by the court under the Fourth Amendment has been beneficial too, but possibly less firm. In Moore v. Student Affairs Committee, it will be recollected, the dean, accompanied by police, entered a student's room without a search warrant because there was a well-founded suspicion that he was harboring marijuana and might escape if warned. Marijuana was found and the student was suspended, but, he claimed, on evidence illegally obtained. The court held that the right of the college to reasonable search took precedence over the student's right to privacy, especially since the student was considered to have given implied assent to the inspection of his quarters. Formerly, of course, no question would have been raised about this priority, but in an era emphasizing civil rights on the campus this priority was not secure without an interpretation of the Fourth Amendment by the court.

Complications commence when the Fourteenth Amendment becomes the occasion for court intervention on the campus. We may begin with the clause in that amendment assuring citizens of the equal protection of the laws. The leading case here has been Missouri *ex rel.* Gaines v. Canada. One of the principal characteristics of any professional group is its control over the qualifications required of its members. In colleges and universities as a matter of expertise the faculty determines entrance and graduation requirements. In the Missouri case, Gaines, a Negro, was denied admission to the University of Missouri law school because of his color. To compensate, Missouri offered to pay his expenses at the law school of a neighboring state, which had a reputable school and which admitted Negroes. Gaines was not satisfied with the alternative and neither was the United States Supreme Court. Consequently the latter intervened in the admissions policy of the University of Missouri, justifying its action on the ground that the university was not giving Gaines the equal protection of the laws.

One may wonder just how far the court is likely to carry this provision on equal protection. Having gone as far as it has, can it stop short of forcing all campuses to provide equal instruction, equal counseling, or equal housing? Some predict just such an egalitarianism.[6] Furthermore, can the Supreme Court affirmation of "one man, one vote" be extended to the campus? The students at Hunter College (New York City) demanded not only representation on college committees but an equal vote! It is not likely that the court will go this far because it has held that the principle of equal protection does not disallow the classification of students into unequal categories as long as the classification is reasonable. Since faculty and students are unequal in scholarly expertise, to treat them equally on most committees would hardly be reasonable. Similarly, if race is an unreasonable classification, can parental income be any less so?

The most controversial clause in the Fourteenth Amendment, repeated from the Fifth, is the guarantee that no one shall be deprived of life, liberty, or property without due process of law. The thrust of this provision is to protect the individual against governmental action, against the federal government in the case of the Fifth Amendment, and against state government in the case of the Fourteenth. Let us note several points on which the demand for due process has arisen on the campus. Foremost is the matter of procedural due process, sometimes called "academic due process." The leading case without doubt is Dixon v. Alabama. There the

[6] Cf. A. E. Wise, "The Constitution and Equal Educational Opportunity," in C. U. Daly (Ed.), *The Quality of Inequality* (Chicago: University of Chicago Press, 1968), pp. 27–46. See also, P. B. Kurland, "Equal Educational Opportunity on the Limits of Constitutional Jurisprudence Undefined," in Daly, *op. cit.*, pp. 47–72.

university took the view that since a student could withdraw from the university at any time and for any reason, so too the university could discontinue the relationship at any time it deemed the relation too unpleasant or difficult. When a student engaged in disruptive activities, the university expelled her without notice, statement of charges, or hearing. The court held that a higher education was much too important in modern life to be denied to a student without at least the rudiments of adversary proceedings. This precedent has been widely followed.

Another aspect of due process is protection of the individual against unreasonable and arbitrary treatment by university officials. The point on which campus autonomy has been most open to suspicion on this score has been the discipline meted out to students who have engaged in disruptive behavior. Interestingly enough, the courts have been somewhat ambivalent about the extent to which due process requires them to intervene in campus discipline, which was long thought to be an internal affair for faculty and administration. In one case, Soglin v. Kaufmann, a student participated in a campus disorder and was suspended for "misconduct." This single word in the university statutes as a cause for suspension seemed to the judge to admit of so great a variety of interpretations that a student could not always reasonably know when he was misconducting himself. Consequently, fearing that the discretion of the university authorities might be exercised capriciously or arbitrarily, the court under guise of ensuring the student due process directed the University of Wisconsin to draw up a list of specifications defining *misconduct*.

In the case of Esteban v. Central Missouri State College, another federal district court took an almost opposite view. Here, too, a student acted contrary to college regulations which admitted some latitude in interpretation, but instead of paring down college autonomy, the judge thought due process was assured by rules which gave the academic authorities some elbow room for discretion. The parent used to have this latitude but with the obsolescence of the old doctrine of *in loco parentis* this custom was no longer a crutch on which to lean. Hence we inevitably face the question, who knows better the considerations relevant to student discipline, the judges or the faculty and deans?

It may come as a surprise that most reviews of the acts of campus officers in the light of civil liberties and the Bill of Rights do not apply to private institutions of higher learning. As I already stated, the Fifth and Fourteenth Amendments are aimed at protecting the individual against governmental action, not against the action of private authorities. For example, some critics thought that the majority in Dixon v. Alabama should have followed the precedent of Anthony v. Syracuse, in which, it will be recalled, the student was dismissed at the pleasure of the university without specification of cause because Syracuse considered attendance a privilege rather than a right. Since Syracuse was a private university the court refused to treat attendance as a right, as it might have if the Fourteenth Amendment had been operative. In a much later case, Greene v. Howard University,[7] the court explicitly refused to apply the Fourteenth Amendment to the student's dismissal because Howard, too, was a private university.

Although not under compulsion to adopt due process, many private institutions have taken a cue from the Alabama case and have voluntarily provided adversary procedures for dismissal cases of both students and faculty. Nevertheless, many think private higher education is the last bastion from which the more unrestricted autonomy of the university can be defended. Yet even this bastion may be undermined if private institutions accept public subsidies leading to the invocation of state action and hence ultimately the Fourteenth Amendment.[8]

Although the necessity for proceeding according to due process is now well-established on public campuses, both judicial and academic anxieties have been expressed on the extent of its impact. From the judicial side the dissenting judge in Dixon v. Alabama expressed alarm that "to extend the injunctive power of federal courts to the problems of day to day dealings between school au-

---

[7] 271 Fed. Supp. 609 (1967).
[8] Cf. E. L. Wilkinson and R. R. Rolapp, "The Private College and Student Discipline," *American Bar Association Journal*, 1970, 56, 121–126.

thority and student discipline and morale is to add to the now crushing responsibilities of federal functionaries the necessity of qualifying as a Gargantuan aggregation of wet nurses or babysitters." On the academic side former President James A. Perkins of Cornell has sounded the tocsin.

Qualitative decisions are the essence of academic life. To replace this kind of decision with either civil laws that must not distinguish between the plumber and the philosopher or with the kind of wrangling over technicalities to which court action can so easily degenerate would do permanent damage not only to the sensitive academic process for judging quality, but indeed to quality itself.

Even more fundamental is the damage that constant legal interference can do to institutional autonomy. Institutional autonomy is the surest guardian of academic freedom. To shift from the rules and procedures that academic institutions have evolved as central to the teaching-learning process and to put academic discipline, appointment, grading, and all manner of educational requirements at the mercy of the courts would mean, quite simply, that civil jurisdiction over intellectual inquiry would be complete. . . .

There are other problems, too, if resort to legal action becomes a campus routine. There are human rights involved in the time and cost of adjudication. Our judicial system is already overloaded. For every hour that might be spent ironing out conflicts on the campus itself, plaintiffs can wait months and sometimes years for action in the courts. Meanwhile, academic careers and perhaps the institution, too, can be ground to a standstill. The costs of legal procedures can be a nightmare for both the individual and the institution. The ACLU budget may not be unlimited. Further there is the damage to the student-teacher relationship. If student and teacher must constantly face the prospect of having to testify against each other, . . . the spark between them dies very quickly.

We cannot let any of this happen. The power to prevent what could easily be the dissolution of all that makes the

143

academy both valuable and unique is still in the hands of the academic community. If this power is to stay there and if this community takes its independence seriously, then every one of its members must bend their energies to keeping the academy intact and preserving its ability to manage its own affairs. At the root of these court cases now upon us is a profound malaise about the direction and purpose of university, multiversity, and indeed the whole educational structure. The courts are simply moving into a vacuum left by a dispersed and weakened community.[9]

Against this view stands that of Clark Byse, a professor of law and a past president of the American Association of University Professors.[10] Sharing Perkins' desire to preserve the autonomy of the university, he nevertheless feels compelled to recognize that unwarranted arbitrariness is not unknown in schools. Without wanting to see a creeping legalism substitute judicial for academic process he pleads for a more jurisprudential understanding of the social significance of due process. Thus Byse does not see due process as a legal octopus with tentacles of inflexibility, obtuseness, conflict, and delay. On the contrary he sees it as an attempt to ensure fair play by taking the circumstances of time and place into account. Indeed, sensitivity to educational considerations is quite clear in the opinion of the majority of the court in Dixon v. Alabama.

The nature of the hearing should vary depending upon the circumstances of the particular case. . . . This is not to imply that a full-dress judicial hearing, with the right to cross-examine witnesses, is required. Such a hearing, with the attending publicity and disturbance of college activities, might be detrimental to the college's educational atmosphere and impractical to carry out. Nevertheless, the rudiments of an adversary procedure may be preserved without encroaching upon the interests of the college.

[9] J. A. Perkins, "The University and Due Process," *Chronicle of the American Council on Education* (Washington, D.C., 1967), pp. 7–9.

[10] C. Byse, "The University and Due Process: A Somewhat Different View," *American Association of University Professors Bulletin,* Summer 1968, 143–148.

Overview

At last we may pause to calculate the overall stance we should take on the relation of the courts and higher education. (a) There seems no doubt that the courts should continue to fulfill their long-standing role of examining whether there is legal authority for whatever acts are taken in the course of the daily life of the academy. (b) There is little disagreement, too, that in general the courts should not examine the discretion exercised under the guise of this authority. The expertise of the courts is the law, not policy in higher education. Yet, perhaps some exceptions to this policy are in order. (c) In the case of the First Amendment the intervention of the courts in university discretion seems to have been warranted and salutary. (d) In the case of measuring university discretion against due process there appears to be ground for reasonable difference of opinion. Probably only time will tell whether Perkins' anxiety will be borne out or will give way to Byse's confidence in the fair play of due process.

Index

147

Index

Curriculum, 103–106; wisdom as a component of, 105

D

Dartmouth College v. *Woodward*, 78–80, 134, 135
Dickey v. *Alabama*, 26–29, 138
Dickson v. *Sitterson*, 63–66
Discipline, rules of, 12–14, 28, 29, 141, 142
Dixon v. *Alabama State Board of Education*, 21–26, 140–142, 144
Domicile, 37–39
Dormitory, 39–45
Double jeopardy, 9, 11
DOYLE, J. E., 13
Due process: procedural, 23–26, 45, 140, 141; protecting against overbreadth of, 14–19, 65, 66, 71–73, 109; substantive, 15, 16, 26

E

Eisen v. *Regents of University of California*, 43, 44
Equal protection of the law, 6, 8, 20, 21, 140
Equality of educational opportunity, 5
Esteb v. *Esteb*, 1–4
Esteban v. *Central Missouri State College*, 17–19, 141
Expectancy of employment, 53–55

F

Faculty: academic freedom of, 57–59, 138; admission of, 140; appointment of, 46–50; dismissal of, 50–55; loyalty oath, 68–75, 138; resignation of, 47; teaching qualifications for, 48–50
Fifth Amendment, 73–75, 138. *See also* Academic freedom
First Amendment, 10, 11, 138, 139

Fourteenth Amendment, 139–142
Fourth Amendment, 139
FRANKFURTER, F., 58, 59, 70, 71
Furner v. *Commissioner of Internal Revenue*, 99, 100

G

Gifts, 96–98
Goldberg v. *Regents of the University of California*, 60–62, 139
Gott v. *Berea*, 89, 90
Greene v. *Howard University*, 142
Grossner v. *Trustees of Columbia University*, 9–12, 139
Guidance, 118–122

H

Hamburger v. *Cornell University*, 124, 125
Hamilton v. *Regents of University of California*, 36, 37
Hammond v. *South Carolina State College*, 12, 13, 138
Hanauer v. *Elkins*, 35, 36
Hartigan v. *Regents of West Virginia University*, 92–94, 134
Hill v. *Commissioner of Internal Revenue*, 98, 99
Higher education: judicial v. academic control of, 53, 92, 104, 109, 110, 136, 137, 143, 144; as a necessity, 2, 3; private, 11, 12, 78–81, 86, 90, 135, 142; as a privilege, 21, 142; proprietary, 110–112, 135; right to, 1–4. *See also* Business
Horace Mann v. *Board of Public Works*, 85–87
HUGHES, C. E., 5–6

I

In locol parentis, 16, 40, 89, 90, 94–96, 139, 141

J

Jay v. *Walla Walla College*, 125
Jones v. *Board of Control*, 55, 56

148

Index

Index